D1106115

WEIRD
FLORIDA

BY
ELIOT
KLEINBERG

Eliot Kleinberg (signature)

LONGSTREET
Atlanta, Georgia

Other Books by Eliot Kleinberg

Pioneers in Paradise: West Palm Beach, The First 100 Years (with Jan Tuckwood); Marietta, Ga., Longstreet Press, 1994

Florida Fun Facts, Sarasota, Pineapple Press, 1995

Historical Traveler's Guide to Florida, Sarasota, Fla., Pineapple Press, 1997

Published by Longstreet
A subsidiary of Cox Newspapers,
A subsidiary of Cox Enterprises, Inc.
2140 Newmarket Parkway
Suite 122
Marietta, Georgia 30067

Printed in the United States of America

1ˢᵗ printing, 1998
Library of Congress Catalog Number 97-76257
ISBN: 1-56352-473-2

Cover Photos:
Alligator: Paul Millette, *Palm Beach Post*
"Floirda,": AP/Wide World Photos

Electronic film prep by OGI, Forest Park, Georgia

Book and jacket design by Burtch B. Hunter

This book is dedicated to the brothers of Pi Lambda Phi Fraternity at the University of Florida, especially Ron "Manl" Mans and Steven "Fish" Aronow. This group taught me to be a man and make friends for life but also displayed weirdness as an art form. They personify Weird Florida.

Eliot Kleinberg
Casa Floridiana
Boca Raton
Winter 1998

ACKNOWLEDGMENTS

Some portions of Weird Florida appeared originally in the *Palm Beach Post*, which has granted permission for their adaptation and republication. *Post* archives have provided many of the photographs contained here.

This book could not have been done without the support of the *Palm Beach Post*, especially managing editor, Tom O'Hara, associate managing editor, Jan Tuckwood, and the talented staff of the *Post* library.

I'm also grateful to columnists John Grogan of the *Sun-Sentinel* in Fort Lauderdale and Frank Cerabino of the *Post*, as well as *Post* staffers Scott Eyman, Scott Hiaasen, Jeff Houck, and Paul Lomartire, who wrote about or tipped me off to many of the bizarre items listed here.

Thanks also to Chuck Shepherd, John J. Kohut, and Roland Sweet, whose *News of the Weird* syndicated series and books partially inspired *Weird Florida* and who gave permission to borrow their idea a little.

And thanks to the many attractions, sites, parks, visitors' bureaus, chambers of commerce, museums and libraries, and their staff and members, many of whom provided incalculable information and guidance.

And to my wife, Debra, who kept my priorities in check, assuring she and my sons were not abandoned while I toiled over *Weird Florida*.

CONTENTS

INTRODUCTION

Florida is the home of more nuttiness per square mile than any place on earth — and we dare the world to prove us wrong. *Weird Florida* is about creepy weirdness, fascinating weirdness, and funny weirdness.

"The Weird Florida Hall of Fame" celebrates Florida's nuttiest people, places, and events of all time.

"History Ain't Pretty: Bloopers, Bozos, and Blunders from Florida's Past" is a roller-coaster ride through five centuries of madness, from Indians mooning soldiers to a state seal that showed mountains.

And "The Daily Weird: Bizarre Florida Behavior from Today's Newspapers" is the kind of stuff you love to find tucked into the back pages of your morning paper. Like the paralyzed guy who didn't know his dog was eating his foot, and the multimillion dollar military jet brought down by pigs.

WHY IS FLORIDA SO WEIRD?

Perhaps it's because it has such a schizophrenic legacy. Settled by Europeans five centuries ago — decades before Plymouth Rock — it has the longest modern history in North America. But at the turn of the twentieth century, Miami was a fishing village of only 900 people. Florida's population has gone from two million people at the beginning of World War II and seven million in 1970 to an estimated 15 million now.

Perhaps it's because Florida naturally drew weird people. Many of its settlers were running away from something. Others saw a quick buck at someone else's expense. And many were just plain nuts and wanted a haven where they could indulge their lunacy.

Perhaps it's just that any time you jam descendants of slaves, rednecks, Indians, con artists, carpetbaggers, drug smugglers, fugitives, UFO abductees, strippers, alligators, and political refugees onto a flat peninsula surrounded by water but with hardly a drop to drink anymore, you get a pretty weird place. Weird Florida.

"Florida, sir, is not worth buying. It is a land of swamps, of quagmires, of frogs and alligators and mosquitoes! A man, sir, would not immigrate into Florida. No, sir! No man would immigrate into Florida—no, not from Hell itself!

—U.S. Rep. John Randolph of Virginia during debate on bringing Florida into the United States

PART I

THE WEIRD FLORIDA HALL OF FAME

UNDYING LOVE

Count Carl Tanzler von Cosel dug up his dead girlfriend, rebuilt her body with chemicals and piano wire, and, well, slept with her for seven years.

He believed his ultraviolet ray machine could restore her. He assembled a wingless plane to fly her into space, where radiation would return her to life. To his own grave, he professed his undying love for someone who was already dead.

This tale of the ultimate in necrophilia tops even Halloween's wild Fantasy Fest in Key West — the town where it all unfolded in the 1930s. And only in Florida could it spawn, six decades later, a musical.

Carl von Cosel: the King of Weird Florida.

"... DORMANT"

In life, von Cosel's love for Elena Milagro Hoyos Mesa was unrequited.

Elena was a dark-eyed Cuban beauty who married young, lost her only child at birth, and was abandoned by her husband. The day she entered the X-ray department at Key West's Marine Hospital, technician Carl von Cosel fell in love. To him, Elena's face was the vision he had seen once in a dream and again on a statue of the Madonna.

"I looked into a face of unearthly beauty, the face of my dreams and visions," he would later write.

Von Cosel, a German immigrant, was 62 in 1931, a gaunt, balding man with a white beard. Von Cosel told people he was born in a haunted family castle in Dresden,

Count Carl von Cosel and his love, Elena

Germany; he boasted nine college degrees and said he was separated for years from his wife and two daughters. He called himself "doctor."

The X ray photographed by von Cosel's own hands told him his dream would die as quickly as it was answered: Elena, only 21, was dying of then-untreatable tuberculosis.

But von Cosel boasted a ray machine he said could restore life.

"The human spirit survives death," he would say. "Life

is dormant, inactive, sleeping in a person who has died."

Soon he was coming by the Hoyos home with his device, along with a prescription of gold dissolved in Elena's drinking water. He bought her jewelry for her birthday, a bed, and food for her family. He accepted pieces of Elena's hair and made masks of her face. When he finally proposed, Elena's father cut him off.

Stricken at the city's Halloween parade, Elena was raced home. Von Cosel showed up with his ray machine for one last desperate attempt. But the love of his life had died at 22.

Elena was buried in a simple grave. Von Cosel, devastated, received the family's permission to move her to a mausoleum. He was horrified to find she had not been embalmed. Her decayed body was covered in maggots and slime. He had an undertaker clean up the remains and place them in the building.

Each night, dressed in black and aided by his cane, he visited the cemetery with the crypt's only key. Each night, he pulled a chair to her coffin to speak to her, write love notes, and leave flowers.

"Ever since the moon began to wane, Elena had begun to sing in her casket with a very soft, clear voice," von Cosel would write later in his memoirs. "'Darling, I would then say, 'very soon the moon will change; the hour approaches when I shall take you home with me.'"

Finally, two years after Elena's death, von Cosel spirited into the graveyard, dragged the coffin back to his wingless plane, and towed the contraption to his home. He locked the door marked "laboratory."

BEESWAX AND PLASTER OF PARIS

Von Cosel had worked on injured faces in World War I, but this was his most daunting effort. Elena's body was barely more than bones.

He imported from Germany one of the world's most powerful antiseptics at $15 an ounce. He produced solutions to restore her body tissues. He packed her in absorbent materials to soak up the chemicals and "rebuilt the lost parts, bandaged the broken parts and replaced the destroyed parts." He strung bones together with piano wire and string. He rebuilt flesh with beeswax and plaster of Paris. He inserted glass eyes and locks of her hair. Her face was cheesecloth and cosmetics. Regularly he would aim the ray machine at her. He soaked her body in a vat and wrapped her in bandages.

He would carry Elena to his bedroom, which was decorated with a death mask of her and a photograph of her in a wedding veil, and lay her in the bed he had given her in life and the one in which she had died. Neighbors would come into his bedroom to hear him play haunting melodies on his pipe organ. None dared peek between the cheesecloth curtains that hid his bed.

Von Cosel had lost his job at the hospital and been forced once to move, but for seven years he bought blue kimonos and silk stockings and shooed away the curious. Elena's sister had heard the whisperings and begged authorities to search von Cosel's home. None would. Finally, nine years after Elena's death and seven years since von Cosel had secretly stolen her body, her sister confronted him. He did not deny her accusations. She came to his bedroom and parted the curtains.

There was Elena, half sitting, her glass eyes staring. She wore a wedding dress and ring.

"That's Elena," the count told her. "I beg you to leave her to me. See how pretty she looks."

The stunned sister gave von Cosel one week to return the body. He would not. She came with deputies. Elena lay in a silk robe, a white rose in her hair.

In one day, the electrifying story of Elena's lover raced through the region, the nation, and even the world. A funeral home placed Elena's body on display; over three days, 6,850 people viewed it. Morticians praised von Cosel's work. But an attorney for the Hoyos family said he was unable to sleep for days, haunted by the image of the count's monstrosity.

Von Cosel's claims of nobility and academic prestige

were quickly discovered to be false. He was declared sane and ordered to stand trial for grave robbing.

Far from being repelled, many people were entranced by the romance. A stranger posted von Cosel's bond. A

Elena's tomb

prominent lawyer volunteered to represent him. A judge's brother wrote a song about the case. Mail from around the country praised him. He was compared to Don Quixote. And money poured in for a fund to entomb Elena in a glass case. Von Cosel, relishing in the limelight, promised to tour the country with the case.

Von Cosel's fans saw only a hopeless romantic. It would be years before they learned the sexual details of the relationship. The doctor brought in to investigate the case would wait until all the Hoyos relatives had died before revealing the facts.

"They said it was a spiritual love, but it was not," a Hoyos family friend said. "He was a necrophile — a lover of the dead. He was a perverted bastard."

A doctor stood beside von Cosel as the body of Elena was examined. It was soft, supple. Her private parts had been reconstructed to allow von Cosel to have sex with her. He had left evidence of their encounters.

". . . CAN I HAVE ELENA BACK NOW?"

The statute of limitations had run out on a grave-robbing charge. As von Cosel was freed, he asked the judge, "Can I have Elena back now?" The appalled judge refused.

Elena's family had her stripped of von Cosel's trappings, chopped up, and buried in the dead of night in a secret grave where he could not find her.

"We were afraid that maniac might come and dig her up again," Police Chief Bienvenido Perez said.

The disconsolate von Cosel was able to give 25-cent tours of his shack and laboratory for six months before interest waned. He resorted to welfare and was finally evicted. One night in 1941, he left in his van for Zephyrhills, a small city north of Tampa, where his sister and wife lived. Another vehicle brought his magic, wingless airplane. Five hours later, an explosion shattered the now-empty tomb he had built for Elena.

The first book version of the Elena affair was called *A Halloween Love Story*. Written by Rod Bethel, son of the cemetery sexton who helped rebury Elena Hoyos, it included reprints of published accounts as well as von Cosel's memoirs.

Key West singer-songwriter Ben Harrison received sick raves for his "Ballad of Maria Elena Hoyos and Count Carl von Cosel," and his idea for a musical play was later transformed into a book, *Undying Love*, published in 1996. The musical of the same name finally began performances in the summer of 1994. Seven artists and three musicians presented it nightly under a banyan tree in the courtyard of a Key West bar.

The count was by then long gone. In 1952, overflowing mail and a strong odor drew a deputy to von Cosel's home. He had been dead perhaps up to three weeks. He was 83. Authorities found his home littered with photo albums filled with pictures of Elena. In the corner was a life-size replica of his forever love.

SOURCES

Bellido, Susana. "Musical Recaps Tale of Count and Corpse," *Miami Herald* (Keys edition), June 24, 1994.

Bethel, Rodman. *A Halloween Love Story*. Oviedo, Fla.: Mickler's Floridiana, 1988.

Capuzzo, Mike. "A Grave Affair," *Tropic Magazine, Miami Herald*, October 25, 1981.

Dorschner, John. "The Love Story of Count von Cosel," *Tropic Magazine, Miami Herald*, March 5, 1972.

Harrison, Ben. *Undying Love*. Key West, Fla.: Duval House Publishing, 1993.

Keith, June. "True Love," *Miami Herald* (Keys edition), October 29, 1994.

Klingener, Nancy. "Undying Love," *Miami Herald*, June 13, 1993.

Mahoney, Lawrence. "Undying Love," *Sunshine Magazine, Fort Lauderdale Sun-Sentinel*, February 21, 1988.

Smiley, Nixon. "Eternal Rest Eluded Elena," *Miami Herald*, July 11, 1965.

THE LOST SQUADRON

Draw a line from the Florida Keys to Puerto Rico, up to the Azores and west to Virginia.

Then stay out.

Florida is more than just one point of the Bermuda Triangle — also called the Devil's Triangle, the Triangle of Death, and the Hoodoo Sea.

Over several centuries, more than 100 ships and planes and 1,000 lives have disappeared into the world's most prominent black hole, actually more a trapezoid than a triangle.

Many left from Florida.

In the Triangle, it is said, compasses go haywire and laws of physics don't apply.

More than 20 books and several movies suggest fishing sloops, lighthouse keepers, and rum runners slid into another dimension, a supernatural vortex, or a time warp, or were nabbed by aliens.

But skeptics have explained away virtually every mystery linked to the Triangle — even Flight 19, the event that sparked the legend.

On December 5, 1945, five Avenger torpedo bombers carrying 14 men left Fort Lauderdale for a routine training mission — Flight 19. They never returned.

A rescue plane with a crew of 13 went after them. It never returned.

A Palm Beach County man may be the region's most infamous modern victim. He spent more than a decade — and his fortune — pursuing the wreckage of the planes that flew into the Bermuda Triangle.

THE LOST SQUADRON

The tale of the Lost Squadron started normally enough, in 1945, at the Fort Lauderdale Naval Air Station, where a young George Bush had trained during World War II. The field is now the Fort Lauderdale-Hollywood International Airport.

Although the war had been over for more than three months, training was still going on.

The five TBM — Torpedo Bomber Medium — Avengers

George Bush, fourth from left in top row, was among those who trained at NAS Fort Lauderdale

on Flight 19 were headed for a mock torpedo run at a wrecked target ship near Bimini. They would head east 77 miles to Great Stirrup Cay, north 84 miles across Grand Bahama Island to Great Sal Cay, then home.

The planes, powered by 1,600-horsepower engines, could go 300 miles per hour. Each carried a crew of three.

One of the squadron members opted not to go on the run. That fifteenth man still doesn't know why.

The planes left about two P.M. on a cool winter day with clear skies. The men expected to get back in time to catch a film at the base theater.

About 3:40 P.M., the time the planes were due back, Lt. Charles Taylor radioed in. By then, the mercurial weather of the subtropics had rapidly deteriorated.

"Both my compasses are out, and I'm trying to find Fort Lauderdale, Florida," he said, "I'm over land, but it's broken. I'm sure I'm in the Keys, but I don't know how far down, and I don't know how to get to Fort Lauderdale."

It appears Taylor meant to aim northeast toward Fort Lauderdale, but in his confusion really headed further out to sea. The squadron followed.

Lt. Cdr. Don Poole, the base's flight training officer, swears he heard one pilot radio, "Damn it, if we would just fly west, we would get home."

Soon the transmissions were growing weaker and the fixes more tenuous.

The Naval Air Station in Opa-locka reported hearing a faint "FT, FT," — the planes' squadron designation — but it was two hours after the planes should have run out of gas.

One ham radio operator later claimed he heard one pilot say, "Don't come after me . . . they look like they're from outer space."

About 150 miles to the north, a PBM Mariner flying boat carrying 13 airmen took off from Banana River Air Station, now Patrick Air Force Base, near Cape Canaveral.

The rescue plane, the first of a massive search mission, had enough fuel to fly 24 hours and was packed with rescue gear and an automatic distress transmitter.

The rescue crew radioed that it had reached the last presumed position of the Avengers, was flying in tight circles, and would call in every three minutes. It radioed once more. Then it, too, vanished.

A merchant ship reported seeing an explosion off Melbourne Beach that might have been the PBM.

More than 242 planes and 18 ships — including an aircraft carrier — spent four days searching 250,000 square miles, and foot parties scoured beaches in Florida and the islands.

Rescuers searched the area for the planes, which were designed to float for 90 seconds while pilots were trained to get out in 60. Planes also carried life rafts. But the waves had been high and the weather brutal.

No sign of the lost planes or their would-be rescuers was ever found.

"This unprecedented peace-time loss seems to be a total mystery, the strangest ever investigated in the annals of Naval investigation," one Navy Board of Inquiry member said.

"They vanished as completely as if they'd flown to Mars," another panel member said dryly, perhaps not realizing the Pandora's box he'd opened.

Suddenly, all those tales of missing ships and planes over the years dropped into place. Everyone claimed to know what happened to those unfortunate pilots.

"They are still here, but in a different dimension of a magnetic phenomenon that could have been set up by a UFO," Miami scientist Manson Valentine told the *Miami News*.

"I have gone through hundreds of reports from ships' captains, pilots and other reliable eyewitnesses, and I am now convinced that extraterrestrial beings on UFOs is the only logical answer," John Wallace Spencer wrote in *Limbo of the Lost*.

"They are being held captive by Atlanteans in huge caverns beneath the Devil's Triangle," Page Bryant concluded in *A Psychic Looks at the Devil's Triangle*.

Even Steven Spielberg got into the act. In his 1978 film "Close Encounters of the Third Kind," the crew of the Avengers was kidnapped by aliens and returned to earth three decades later; they had not aged a day.

THE TRIANGLE SOLVED

Critics are blunt.

They say the two biggest demons in the Devil's Triangle are environmental factors and pilot error.

The earth's magnetic north pole is not at the actual pole, and the variations between the two can cause a discrepancy of as much as 20 degrees. The Triangle is one of two places on earth where a magnetic compass points to the true north pole; the other is the Devil's Sea off Japan. This could confuse pilots and ship captains into losing their way.

Some scientists suggested the confluence of magnetic forces could have actually caused air turbulence that tore the planes apart. But they don't explain the loss of the ships.

A more mundane explanation is the presence in the Triangle of the Gulf Stream, the swift, unpredictable current running through the Atlantic that has torn up many ships and spawned storms that did the same.

Critics also point to human error; many a pilot or boat captain overextended his skills in tackling the open ocean.

In *The Bermuda Mystery Solved*, Arizona researcher Lawrence David Kische painstakingly investigated each disappearance, studying newspaper clippings and investigative reports. He showed how many accounts, embellished over the years, conveniently omitted explanations for the incidents — especially bad weather — or twisted facts to fit the legend.

The pragmatic explanation for the doomed Avengers has been that the pilots became disoriented in a driving rain and simply ran out of gas, ditching into the ocean. The pilots, rocking in the 40-knot winds and 14-foot seas, may never have gotten out of their planes.

In fact, testimony would indicate that, at the point the pilots concluded they were lost, they were right on course.

The possible explosion of the PBM was said to have taken place three hours after takeoff; it actually occurred 23 minutes after takeoff, at about the spot where the rescue plane would be.

THE LAST VICTIM?

In May 1991, divers searching for sunken Spanish treasure ships found the wreckage of five Avengers 750 feet down and about 10 miles from Fort Lauderdale.

The only problem: the Navy concluded they were five different Avengers. A researcher said they were from various missions and just happened to plunk into the water near each other.

In fact, 139 Avengers were lost off the Florida coast during World War II — a high statistic for accidental downings that didn't say much for the quality of the Avengers but gave weight to the skeptics.

These skeptics included Jon Myhre, a decorated former Vietnam pilot and air traffic controller who spent $100,000 of his money chasing the Lost Squadron.

He began his journey in 1982. After studying 500 pages of navy investigation reports and lost pilots' radio logs and laying out charts, he set out an argument that the planes got turned around and thought they were in the Keys when they were in the Abaco Islands of the Bahamas. As they continued north, they ended up ditching off New Smyrna Beach.

It was the Challenger disaster in January 1986 that gave Myhre his break. Underwater searches for the space shuttle's wreckage spotted a small plane on the ocean floor.

By 1989, Myhre had quit his job and was chasing the planes full time. Files and documents packed his small trailer.

In 1991, Myhre and two business partners announced they had recovered all but the tail section of an Avenger 390 feet down and 30 miles north of Cape Canaveral. Myhre said it was FT-117, the first of the planes to ditch.

It was just two miles from where Myhre had calculated

it would be.

Health problems slowed Myhre down. He finally ran out of money and had to abandon his life's dream.

"I've found the answer to something that's considered to be the world's greatest mystery," he said in a fiftieth-anniversary article in December 1995. "I have the data to back up what I say. And nobody cares."

OTHER FLORIDA-BASED DISAPPEARANCES IN THE BERMUDA TRIANGLE

✗ 1909: *The Spray*, a 37-foot yawl with adventurer Joshua Slocum aboard for an around-the-world attempt, disappeared south of Miami.

✗ October 1944: Cuban freighter *Rubicon*, found by Coast Guard in Gulf Stream off Palm Beach, deserted except for dog.

✗ July 1947: A U.S. Army Superfortress bomber with a crew of six, headed from Bermuda to Morrison Army Air Field in West Palm Beach, disappeared 100 miles off Bermuda.

✗ March 1948: Famed jockey Al Snider and two friends anchored their cruiser off the upper Keys and rowed a short distance away to fish but never returned. Boat later found empty.

✗ December 1948: A DC-3 with 30 passengers and crew chartered to fly from San Juan to Miami, disappeared over the Keys.

✗ June 1950: *Sandra*, a 350-foot freighter traveling from Savannah to Puerto Cabello, Venezuela, with 11 aboard, disappeared off St. Augustine.

✗ December 1954: The 3,337-ton converted navy ship *Southern Districts* was lost in the Straits of Florida with 22 aboard.

✗ January 1958: A 46-foot racing yacht, *Revonoc*, with millionaire publisher Harvey Conover and crew of four aboard, disappeared within sight of land off the upper Keys.

✗ February 1963: The 425-foot *Marine Sulphur Queen*, with

a crew of 39, on its way from Norfolk, Virginia, to Beaumont, Texas, vanished near Dry Tortugas.

✗ August 1963: The first jets lost to the Triangle were two new KC-135 tanker planes from Homestead Air Force Base, with a total of 11 aboard, that disappeared 200 miles southwest of Bermuda.

✗ June 1965: C-119 *Flying Boxcar*, with a crew of 10, on the way from Homestead Air Force Base to Grand Turk Island, Bahamas, disappeared about 100 miles from Grand Turk.

✗ January 1967: A Chase YC-22 cargo plane with four aboard, involved in the filming of a sea movie, disappeared between Fort Lauderdale and Bimini.

✗ December 1967: Cabin cruiser *Witchcraft* with two aboard was last seen at buoy one mile off Miami.

✗ November 1970: *The Piper Comanche* was lost between West Palm Beach and Jamaica with three aboard.

SOURCES

Associated Press. "Navy to Claim 5 Avenger Planes Off Fort Lauderdale," *Palm Beach Post*, May 22, 1991.

Associated Press. "New Mysteries Found With Lost Planes," *Palm Beach Post*, May 19, 1991.

Berlitz, Charles. *The Bermuda Triangle*. New York: Doubleday and Co., 1974.

Fernandez, John. "Bermuda Triangle 'Lost Patrol' is Missing — Again," *Palm Beach Post*, June 5, 1991.

Fernandez, John. "New Angle on 'Devil's Triangle'," *Palm Beach Post*, May 17, 1991.

Kaye, Ken. "50 Years After the Lost Patrol," *Fort Lauderdale Sun-Sentinel*, December 3, 1995.

Kleinberg, Howard. "Give It Up — They're Forever Lost," *Palm Beach Post*, June 10, 1991.

Kusche, Lawrence David. *The Bermuda Triangle Mystery – Solved*. New York: Harper and Row, 1975.

O'Meilia, Tim. "Search for Flight 19 May Be Grounded," *Palm Beach Post*, October 1, 1990.

Pounds, Stephen. " 'Lost Patrol' Plane Found, Lantana Man Says," *Palm Beach Post*, September 10, 1991.

Winer, Richard. "Legend of the Lost Patrol," *Sunshine Magazine*, *Fort Lauderdale Sun Sentinel*, December 1, 1985.

OTHER MYSTERIES OFF FLORIDA'S COAST

THE PYRAMID
Alfred Conway of Vero Beach claimed to have found a 30-foot-tall underwater pyramid in less than 100 feet of water off Indian River County. Such a structure would be at least 2,000 years older than all other known pyramids, including those in Egypt and Central America. But archaeologists were skeptical because Conway could not mark the exact location. In 1985 he saw what appeared from the air to be the top of a pyramid. He dropped a buoy within several hundred yards the next day but couldn't see anything from a boat. Conway saw it a second time from the air, but when he tried to drop another buoy, a line tangled in the plane's stabilizer, forcing him to land. Conway described the structure as a stair pyramid at least 30 feet tall, with a base about 86 feet long on each of four sides. He claimed to have seen the outline of two other structures nearby that he described as O-shaped and L-shaped.

Hamburg, Jay. "The 8th Wonder of the World? Vero man lays claim to underwater pyramid," *Orlando Sentinel*, March 15, 1987.

AMELIA EARHART'S LAST STOP
Amelia Earhart came to Miami in May 1937 on the last American stop of her around-the-world trip. She was visiting her stepson. While there, she decided to start the overseas leg from Miami and head east, instead of going west from Oakland. She left June 1, on a route to Puerto

Palm Beach Post

Amelia Earhart's fateful flight left from South Florida.

Rico, Brazil, Dakar, India, Java, America's west coast, and, finally, New York. On July 2, near Howland Island along the equator in the Pacific, she radioed she was nearly out of gas. She was never heard from again.

Kleinberg, Howard. "Earhart's Last Flight Began Here," *Miami News*, August 18, 1984.

WHAT HAPPENED TO ALEXANDER RORKE?
The disappearance of Alexander Rorke, 37, and Geoffrey Sullivan, 28, may well be at human hands rather than the supernatural. Rorke, a freelance journalist and loose-cannon operative, took part in a failed bombing raid on Cuba in April 1963. Later that year, in the Bahamas, the British government seized his boat.

One of those connected to Rorke was Frank Fiorini, later identified as Frank Sturgis, one of the Cubans caught red-handed in 1974 in the Watergate office complex.

"Frank Fiorini was not employed by the CIA in 1960, nor was Alex Rorke," Neill Macaulay, professor of history at the University of Florida, wrote to *Latin American Newsletters* in July 1976. "I knew them in Miami in 1960 and they were strictly freelancers. The CIA avoided them like the plague. While the CIA has engaged in comparably evil and/or stupid activities, it's not responsible for this particular caper."

In November 1963, the plane carrying Rorke and piloted by Sullivan left South Florida, presumably for Central America. It vanished in the Caribbean; neither was ever found. A $25,000 reward by Rorke's wealthy father, a former New York district attorney, was fruitless.

Sullivan's daughter, who was seven when he disappeared, is now a private investigator in Maine and spent more than a decade collecting hundreds of documents, most of them spotted with blacked-out sections and indications of hundreds more pages still withheld for reasons of national security.

In a segment for the television program "Unsolved Mysteries," Sherry Sullivan said a man told her he saw Rorke and Sullivan in Belize two days after they disappeared. And a journalist said a man in Cuba told him he had been in prison with the two men. And Frank Sturgis, who died in December 1993, said Rorke intended to fly to Nicaragua to convince its government to supply freelance bombing missions to Cuba.

Flamboyant Miami attorney Ellis Rubin, who represented various Cuban exile groups, said in February 1994 that he organized a search party for Rorke.

"He either went down at sea or in the mountains or was secretly executed," Rubin said.

"I'd like to know, too," Marita Lorenz said in 1994, shortly after publication of her book, *Marita*, in which she claimed to have been Fidel Castro's mistress and that she chickened out at the last minute in an assassination attempt on the dictator.

Rorke, Lorenz claims, was a loose cannon who went on clandestine CIA raids into Cuba and may have taken too many pictures. She doesn't believe he was captured and jailed or that he was actually a Castro agent.

"It's just hanging unsolved," Lorenz said. "It shouldn't be. Someone knows the answer. And the answer must be in Florida."

"CIA Secrets," *Unsolved Mysteries.*

Interview with Marita Lorenz, February 1994.

Interview with Ellis Rubin, February 1994.

Lorenz, Marita. *Marita.* New York: Thunder's Mouth Press, 1993.

THE GHOST OF FLIGHT 401

The flight engineer of an Eastern Airlines flight from Atlanta to Miami was surprised to find a uniformed crew member already sitting at his seat.

"You don't need to worry about the preflight," the stranger said. "I've already done it."

Then the man simply vanished.

The engineer had recognized the stranger. It was flight engineer Don Repo. Repo was dead.

The 52-year-old was one of 101 people who'd died December 29, 1972, when Eastern Flight 401, packed with holiday travelers, slammed into the Everglades 19 miles northwest of Miami International Airport. Another 75 miraculously survived. At the time, it was the nation's deadliest single-plane accident. Investigators determined that while the crew was distracted with front landing gear, the plane quietly coasted to its destruction.

In the years that followed, stories swirled about flight crews, attendants, and passengers who swore to several sightings of Repo and Capt. Bob Loft on Eastern planes. It was theorized that the two appeared to warn of impending problems in an effort to assuage their guilt over their fatal mistake.

Author John Fuller collected the tales in his 1976 book, *The Ghost of Flight 401*, later made into a 1978 TV film by

Jay Repo

Did Don Repo haunt Eastern planes?

the same name, starring Ernest Borgnine as Repo, the ill-fated engineer trying to atone for the last few minutes of his life.

"There was never anything to it," says Jim Ashlock, who ran public relations for Eastern from 1966 until it folded in 1991. With Eastern as dead and buried as the pilots and passengers on Flight 401, he has no motivation to lie now, he claims.

"My position hasn't changed a lick in 20 years," says Ashlock, now head of the Tallahassee Chamber of Commerce. "Fuller made that whole thing up. Anybody like that has to infer that there's some kind of conspiracy."

He says Eastern hid no logs, destroyed no documents, intimidated no witnesses.

"I still have my natural reporter's curiosity," the former newspaperman says. "I actually would talk to folks. I talked to flight attendants. I said, 'Who? Tell me where? Let me find out about it.' You can never track back to anything of any substance. That's why I put it in the category of the Flying Dutchman. In this case it didn't hold water."

Ashlock notes most of the reports in the book are second hand; those that aren't came from people whose real names Fuller did not use.

In the book, Fuller swore by the stories witnesses told him directly. And he argued there were too many stories, with too many specifics, for this to be all legend.

Jay Repo believes.

Repo, one of four siblings, was a teenager when his father's plane dropped into the Everglades. He was a student at Florida State University in 1974 when John Fuller called him to say he'd contacted his dead father.

For proof, Fuller told Jay about a novelty bank that the boy kept in his room that read "barrel of money." Jay still has that barrel, and he doesn't know how Fuller could know about it.

"I'm not really into the supernatural," Jay Repo said in a November 1997 interview. "I think what really happened was that once in a while someone gets killed that really wants to live. For some reason they don't want to move on, and they stick around and somehow communicate to people that are living."

Repo does dispute that his father's ghostly acts are those of a guilty man. In the few days Don Repo lingered, Jay says, he told his family he believed he'd been in a midair collision.

"I'm a businessman," says the Deerfield Beach restaurant food salesman. "I'm not a Jesus freak or into mythology or seances. But the things that happened are so astronomical."

NO ONE HEARD THE CHIME

Flight 401 from New York's John F. Kennedy International Airport was a new Lockheed L-1011 Tri-Star, the $20-million Cadillac of the Eastern fleet, and the first of the jumbo jets to crash.

As it approached Miami International, the crew lowered the landing wheels. But a tiny green $12 light indicated the front wheel wasn't down.

The pilot decided to make another circle while the crew

checked the gear. In the next 10 minutes, investigators would conclude, an incredible sequence of snafus added up to disaster. The autopilot was somehow deactivated — perhaps from a pilot bumping the steering column.

The warning chime that the plane was descending below 2,000 feet went off next to Repo's chair. But it was too soft to be heard above the din of the plane.

Plus, no one was there to hear it. Most of the flight crew, including Repo, was jammed down into the cockpit's "hellhole," checking the landing gear.

And, with city lights miles away, anyone looking out a window would have been unable to discern between the moonless night and the jet-black swamp below.

The crash would prompt industry changes, including better altitude-warning and ground-clearance systems. And pilots were taught to always have at least one of them flying the plane.

A former wildlife officer in the swamp for a late-night frog-gigging expedition, saw the flash as two fuel tanks burst open. So did passing pilots, who immediately alerted authorities.

But the crash site was so remote — eight miles north of Tamiami Trail and 100 nearly impassable yards of swamp and muck from a canal levee — that rescue efforts were laborious.

The water had doused the flames, and the plane had split apart as it pancaked into the swamp and scattered 1,600 feet.

Workers staggered through knee-deep water to carry the injured to overflowing choppers and airboats.

It would be sunrise before all the survivors had been moved and workers could begin the grisly work of removing bodies.

Back at the airport, Sadie Messina, waiting for her husband to arrive on Flight 401, heard a little whistle. It was a signal he used as a family code. Her two sons heard it, too. They turned to look. He wasn't there.

At that moment, Messina would say later, she knew her

husband was dead. It was the exact moment the plane went down.

The eerie fallout had just begun.

"MY GOD. IT'S BOB LOFT."

According to Fuller's book, within three months of the crash of Flight 401, the sightings began — always on L-1011s and nearly always on airplane #318. By the end of 1973, nearly every airline employee in the United States had heard about them.

Fuller claims Eastern management denied the incidents, and there are no official reports to support them. Employees would not come forward for fear they'd be sent to the nut house. Flight log pages detailing incidents were torn out.

"You're operating a highly technical vehicle in interstate commerce," Ashlock responds. "Anything abnormal in the operation in that vehicle has to be logged. There were no missing log entries. You'd have the FAA all over you so fast you'd have your hair stand up. They'd tear you to pieces."

The alleged incidents on airplane #318:

✗ An unexplainable cold was felt in galleys, despite near-by ovens.

✗ A cloud of condensation in the galley formed clearly into the face of a man with dark hair, gray sideburns, and steel-rimmed glasses — a face similar to that of Don Repo.

✗ As a flight from Newark to Miami prepared to depart, a flight attendant noted her head count was off. She soon saw why: a man in an Eastern captain's uniform was sitting in first class. No captains had signed to "dead-head" on the flight; those who do ride in a jump seat, not with passengers. She questioned him, but he stared straight ahead, ignoring her and another attendant who walked up. As the two-and-a-half-dozen curious passengers watched, the pilot came back to the cabin, froze, and said, "My God. It's Bob Loft." Then the man just vanished. The plane was delayed and searched. It finally took off, this time with a shaken crew but the right passenger count.

✗ Marriott caterers loading food into the galley saw a flight engineer vanish in front of them. There was a lengthy delay before they could be persuaded to continue the loading.

✗ As a flight from New York approached the Everglades, a male voice on the public address system gave the usual "fasten-seat-belts, no-smoking" announcement. The crew said no one was using the PA at that moment.

✗ A flight engineer on an Atlanta-to-Miami run heard a loud knocking in the "hellhole," went below and saw nothing. He turned to see Repo's face in the cockpit control panel.

✗ A woman in first class noticed that the Eastern flight engineer seated beside her seemed pale. He would not respond to her. Flight attendants and several passengers saw the man disappear. They later identified the man as Repo.

Some claimed all the sightings were on L-1011s that contained parts salvaged from the aircraft that crashed. At one point, the airline reportedly began removing the parts.

"You had to reach out and infer that there's some kind of spiritual attachment even to nuts and bolts," Jim Ashlock says. "The parts were not put in other airplanes. They were all confiscated by the FAA for a long period."

Sightings on other aircraft, as recounted by Fuller:

✗ An Eastern vice president boarded a plane at JFK, stopped to say hello to a captain in first class, and recognized him as Loft. The captain disappeared.

✗ A flight attendant on a New York-to-Miami run opened an overheard bin and saw Loft's face.

✗ An attendant in Miami opened a galley door and saw Repo's face.

✘ A mechanic in a bay couldn't find his screwdriver. He held his arms out, palms up, in frustration. His screwdriver was slapped into his hand. No one else was there.

✘ An attendant discovered an overloaded circuit on a galley oven. A man in an engineer's uniform appeared. Later, the only engineer on the plane arrived. The attendant looked up Repo's photograph and identified it as that of the first engineer to the galley.

✘ A woman on an Eastern plane leased to TWA for the summer began screaming and said a man had suddenly materialized in the seat beside her.

"WE WILL NOT LET IT HAPPEN"

Soon the Loft sightings began to fade, while those of Repo increased. Witnesses said he seemed to be trying to help with the plane. Some pilots actually requested aircraft #318, believing it under special protection.

✘ Two attendants and a flight engineer on a New York-to-Mexico City flight, on aircraft #318, saw Repo's face reflected in an oven window. It said, "Watch out for fire on this airplane," then vanished. The plane landed safely in Mexico City, but as it restarted to continue to Acapulco, engine three would not start. The plane was taken out of service and a crew prepared to fly it back to Miami on two engines, for repairs. But just after takeoff, at only 50 feet, engine one stalled and backfired. The plane circled on the last working engine and landed.

✘ A captain was warned about an electrical fire by a flight engineer riding in the jump seat. The captain called for a recheck and the crew found a faulty circuit. The crew later identified the man as Repo.

✘ A captain came off a San Juan flight and described a direct encounter with Repo, who told him, "There will never be another crash of an L-1011 . . . we will not let it happen."

SOUL RESCUES

In *The Ghost of Flight 401*, a pilot — convinced that Repo

was trapped between death and the afterlife, not realizing he was dead or racked with guilt or both — conducted, in plane #318's galley, an exorcism, a deliverance of Repo to the Great Beyond.

As he sprinkled blessed water, he felt a chilling cold and a stiff wind. A shape formed. He told it, "Don't you know you are dead?"

Invoking the name of Jesus Christ, he called an angel of light to lead Repo to where he belonged. A bright light blinded him, and the apparition was gone.

Fuller also says he participated in two different Ouija-board sessions during which he says he communicated with Repo. In a third, he was accompanied by Repo's wife, he says.

As for Repo's promise that an L-1011 will never crash again, Ashlock says, "tell that to Delta." It was a Delta L-1011, flying from Fort Lauderdale–Hollywood International Airport, that crashed in July 1985 at Dallas–Fort Worth International Airport, killing 137 people.

Ashlock insists he'd rather the stories were true.

"My Lord," he says. "It would be kind of nice to have someone tell us exactly what happened in the accident.

"And can you imagine . . . here we would be on the threshold of the greatest breakthrough in mankind, reaching the other side. If I could have found a way at the time to prove there had been communication with the other world, I probably would have been the most famous public relations man in the world."

EPILOGUE

Don Repo's hauntings did not end with that "exorcism" in the belly of an airplane, his son says.

Jay Repo says he got a chill when a hotel clerk in Europe inexplicably placed him in room 401 and the time a disc jockey at a Zurmatt, Switzerland, bar played "Mack the Knife" — his father's favorite song.

He tells of how his mother asked for a sign as she drove to a daughter's nursing-school graduation at Florida

State. He says she asked to see a bird.

"Right in the middle of the commencement address, there's this damn bird. It's flying in the middle of the Civic Center. It stopped the speech. Coincidence? Could be."

Jay Repo says his father came to him even on his wedding night. As he and his new bride entered their sparkling-clean room at a Miami hotel, one they hadn't told anyone they'd chosen, they opened the empty closet. On the floor was a pair of plastic Eastern Airline wings.

SOURCES

Cone, Tracie. "Unexplained Events Become More Haunting at Halloween," *Miami Herald*, October 30, 1992.

Fuller, John. *The Ghost of Flight 401*. New York: Berkley Publishing Corp., 1976.

Interview with Jay Repo, November 26, 1997.

Kaye, Ken. "Flight 401," *Fort Lauderdale Sun-Sentinel*, December 29, 1992.

Maltin, Leonard. *TV Movies and Video Guide*. New York: New American Library, 1990 Edition.

Markowitz, Arnold. "The Crash of Flight 401 20 Years Later," *Miami Herald*, December 29, 1992.

OTHER FLORIDA GHOSTS

KEY WEST:

✗ Fort Zachary Taylor: Volunteers say ghosts have made brief appearances, whistled, howled, even sang "Dixie." One said a ghost told him where to find buried artifacts.

✗ The Artist House: A psychic said a little girl sits on the staircase in a white old-style nightgown. About five years old with long, light brown curls, she seems to be very angry about something. A doll in the house, made in 1903 to resemble a little boy who would later own the house for decades, was said to giggle or end up in different parts of the house with no explanation. Pictures came off the wall. Doors locked inexplicably. A bookcase door flew open.

✗ The Audubon House: Built in 1830, it honors the great naturalist, although he never lived there. The house fell to neglect and in 1958 was scheduled for razing but was saved. It became a museum run by the National Audubon Society. Now, Audubon's ghost supposedly haunts the place. A guest said he was standing on the porch when he saw a man in nineteenth-century garb — long jacket, ruffled shirt, slim trousers. Recently, a mysterious doll brought attention to the home. Lightbulbs were found unscrewed. Passersby outside looked into windows of locked rooms and saw ethereal figures dancing. And a photograph of the doll had a strange black slash through it. The doll later vanished.

Florida Keys Tourist Development Council

Does Audobon haunt his home?

MIAMI-DADE COUNTY:

✗ At a Miami house that served as the first Cuban embassy, people report seeing an apparition of a woman dressed for a party.

✗ Miami's historic Vizcaya mansion is reportedly haunted by a caretaker.

✗ At Miami's Club Alhambra Apartments, a disembodied arm jiggled doorknobs, waved a white cloth, and painted pictures on a living room wall.

✗ At a Miami home where a woman shot her husband as he beat their son, tenants said for years that they heard crashing sounds, felt an unseen presence, and smelled a stench.

✗ Among the ghosts at Coral Gables' Biltmore Hotel is that of gang hit man Thomas "Fats" Walsh, cut down March 7, 1929, in the thirteenth-floor gambling suite.

✗ Even before fashion designer Gianni Versace was slain, his Miami Beach home reportedly was visited by the spirits of Al Capone and Harry Houdini.

✗ No less than 224 documented incidents occurred at Tropication Arts, a wholesale novelty warehouse, starting on December 15, 1955.

First, several glass steins were discovered broken. Then mugs, combs, fans, and other items began rolling off shelves. "Ghostologist" Suzy Smith said she recorded 300 separate incidents over 24 days; boxes containing dozens of items leaped from shelves and crashed to the ground, spilling their contents. Skeptical at first, Smith contacted the head of the Psychical Research Foundation at Durham, North Carolina. By then, print and broadcast reporters were crawling over Tropication Arts.

The first police officer had seen so many strange events in the first hour that he called for backup, telling a superior, "There's something mighty strange going on."

"Well, can't you save me a trip and tell me about it on the phone?" the sergeant asked. The officer said he couldn't.

One logical explanation after another was eliminated. A cynical magician was convinced when he saw two boxes, each weighing four pounds, drop to the floor, landing perfectly on top of each other.

Finally a medium who was the future father-in-law of one employee performed an exorcism. The embarrassed worker, Julio Vazquez, didn't come to work the next day. That day, nothing fell. When he returned, things started happening again.

That's when suspicion began to center around the 19-year-old Cuban immigrant. Investigators later determined Vazquez' personal problems were somehow manifested in bursts of psychic power. One night, he broke in and stole some cash and was fired. That day, the activity stopped. The psychic researchers later flew the young man to North Carolina in order to study his possible powers.

BROWARD COUNTY:
✗ In 1993, the Cahows of Dania said they experienced a bright light, a dramatic temperature drop, and the smell of chlorine in their daughter's bedroom. Within a week, the light had taken the shape of a hooded figure. They said a neighbor also felt someone or something prowling her apartment.

✗ Also that year, a Pompano Beach family said they shared their home with the ghost of a thin, shy 11-year-old who fled when encountered.

✗ Linda Mitchell of Hollywood said suitcases fell off her shelf, and her husband saw a woman in early 1900s dress float from the attic into her daughter's bedroom. Mr. Mitchell later saw a girl about six years old calling, "Mama." Each apparition sent the family rottweiler into a frenzy. The family reported 10 incidents in three years. They said it stopped after a dalmatian the Mitchells had owned only a month tore up their daughter's face, forcing them to put the dog to sleep. They suspected the dog was possessed and took the ghosts with him.

✗ In 1981, Linda Koenig had lost her two-and-a-half-year-old daughter to a rare form of cancer. She told her husband she'd love to have a sign that her girl was in a better place — perhaps the lights could go out for 10 seconds. It happened. Her husband also told her she wouldn't get pregnant again until she'd gotten past Laurie's death. Six years later, when she finally got rid of the last of Laurie's things, it happened. Her new son had the same line on his chest that had been on his sister's chest.

PALM BEACH COUNTY:

✗ A night watchman at Whitehall, the palatial Palm Beach home of Florida pioneer developer Henry Flagler that was later turned into a hotel, swore several years ago that he had a chat with Flagler at four one morning. A cleaning lady said she was slapped in the rear, turned, and saw no one. Doors wouldn't open. One guest found her Timex stopped every time she was in the hotel. A set of plates was locked in a glass cabinet; one was found cracked; another cracked the next day, and a third with a bullet hole. A set of silver asparagus tongs had been moved two shelves down.

Miami News

Does pioneer Henry Flagler haunt his former home?

✗ At one Palm Beach estate, people reported hearing howling winds on calm days.

✗ At Phipps Plaza, a naked lady supposedly runs through the courtyard.

✗ Muriel McCormick, a former stage actress who later founded the Palm Beach Playhouse, once took part in a "spiritual marriage" when she wed the ghost of Lt. G. Alexander McKinlock, the son of a Palm Beach grande dame.

✗ At the Lake Worth Playhouse, the ghost of Lucian Oakley — the theater's cofounder, who killed himself — is said to blast cold air at visitors, move heavy objects, and leave a giant handprint on walls.

✗ A manager, two assistant managers, and a janitor at a Royal Palm Beach Burger King claim to have seen an apparition of a young man who disappeared in front of them.

MARTIN COUNTY:

✗ In the housekeeper's residence at Gilbert's Bar House of Refuge, near Stuart on Hutchinson Island, people have seen faces at the upstairs windows and sparkles in the downstairs bedroom and inexplicably smelled beef stew.

CENTRAL FLORIDA:

✗ At Ashley's Restaurant in Rockledge, dozens of patrons and employees claim to have seen a young girl in roaring-twenties garb emerge from a restroom stall or appear in a mirror. The ghost is believed to have been a woman murdered in the 1930s in a storage room there.

✗ A ghost said to haunt a Victorian home in Clermont finally moved on after its story appeared on the national television show "Unsolved Mysteries." The crew came to do a segment on what was then the city's only unsolved killing — the 1975 shooting of a man in the driveway at the house. Police reports said Clermont

High School graduate John Harden, 32, was killed with a 20-gauge shotgun at close range the night of March 22, 1975, while he was trying to put out a fire inside his truck. Telephone lines to the home were cut, leading police to believe the fire was set to lure Harden outside. Current and former owners described apparitions, told of hearing footsteps when no one else was present, and of having music boxes begin playing spontaneously.

✗ At the Old Bradford House in Ocklawaha — the home where gangster moll Ma Barker and her son died in a shoot-out with FBI agents in 1935 — strange footsteps, the sounds of card-playing, and the vision of a woman combing her hair have been seen.

SEBRING:

✗ Mr. Parker, a former manager of Kenilworth Lodge who died in the 1950s, is said to haunt the place. Some staffers swear furniture, doors, and air-conditioning knobs move, and taps are heard on doors from inside empty rooms.

TAMPA:

✗ Projectionist Foster "Fink" Finley worked at the venerable Tampa Theatre from 1930 until he died in his booth of a heart attack in December 1965. Employees later swore Finley's ghost inhabited the place. One employee said his lost knife suddenly showed up at a place where he'd already looked, an unseen finger tapped his shoulder, and phantom chains rattled through the building.

NORTHEAST FLORIDA:

✗ St. Augustine's many spooks prompted nightly walking tours and a book, *Ghosts of St. Augustine*, by Dave Lapham of Orlando, which documents two dozen tales from America's oldest city. The 300-year-old home of Pat and Maggie Patterson contains the ghosts of a seventeenth-century Spanish governor, a sentry, a calico cat, and a shadowy white figure. The apparitions like to turn on lights, hide jewelry, and move furniture, the

Is historic Castillo de San Marcos haunted?

owners say. Other hauntings include the Ponce de Leon Hotel by its founder, Henry Flagler, who is also known to haunt the Castillo de San Marcos, the lighthouse, inns, two downtown historic cemeteries, and homes.

✗ Sailors aboard the aircraft carrier USS *Forrestal*, based at Naval Air Station Jacksonville, claim to have encountered a poltergeist called "George" who causes flickering lights, voices on disconnected telephones, and unexplained whistling and footsteps. Some said he was the ghost of one of the 134 killed in a 1967 fire aboard the ship off the coast of Vietnam. Others said he was a pilot whose body was temporarily placed in a cold-storage box in the hold. One sailor said he answered a telephone and heard a faint voice say "Help! Help! I'm on the sixth deck!"

✗ At Fernandina Beach's Fort Clinch, reenactors who portray Civil War soldiers at the unfinished fort claim to have heard the wail of a baby and the disembodied clomping of boots. Two volunteers swear they saw four ghostly figures in Civil War garb walk across the parade grounds and up a ramp and disappear.

MONTICELLO:

✘ After the death of his wife, Confederate surgeon Dr. Thomas Palmer shot himself to death on the third floor of Palmer Place, now a bed-and-breakfast inn. Residents report lights turning on and off by themselves, footsteps in the halls, and sometimes an unearthly image at the end of a hall.

SOURCES

Associated Press, October 29, 1997.

Fort Lauderdale Sun-Sentinel, October 31, 1993.

Hauck, Dennis William. The National Directory of Haunted Places. Sacramento, Cali.: Athanor Press, 1994.

Historical Society of Palm Beach County.

Myers, Arthur. A Ghosthunter's Guide. Chicago: Contemporary Books, 1993.

Orlando Sentinel, October 30, 1992.

Palm Beach Post, June 24, 1994; May 14, 1995; October 31, 1997; November 30, 1997.

Scott, Beth, Norman, and Michael. Haunted America. New York: Tom Doherty Associates, 1994.

Smith, Suzy. Prominent American Ghosts. Cleveland, Oh.: World Publishing, 1967.

St. Petersburg Times, August 7, 1988.

Sunshine Magazine, Fort Lauderdale Sun-Sentinel, October 26, 1977.

FLAME ON

At eight o'clock on a summer morning, a telegram arrived for Mary Hardy Reeser.

The St. Petersburg widow's landlady carried it to her door and knocked three times. When there was no answer, she tried the knob.

It was burning hot.

Two nearby painters came and opened the door; a blast of hot air rushed out.

In the middle of the studio apartment, surrounded by a charred circle, an overstuffed chair was burned down to its springs. The ceiling was stained with soot.

Police found Mary Reeser's head — shriveled to the size of a baseball — along with a small piece of her spine and part of a foot.

That was it.

The 67-year-old woman's death, sometime overnight between July 1 and 2, 1951, is one of the most famous cases ever of alleged spontaneous human combustion — the centuries-old idea of a body inexplicably bursting into flame and burning furiously on its own oils.

Reeser has been dubbed "The Cinder Woman." The simplest explanation was that sedatives Reeser had taken knocked her out, and a dropped cigarette ash set her afire.

But, critics asked, how could a 170-pound woman and

a 70-pound floor lamp be reduced to 10 pounds of ash in an otherwise mostly undamaged apartment? How could a woman be consumed so completely and the fire burn only the tiny circle around her?

"As I review it, the short hairs on the back of my neck bristle with vague fear," Wilton M. Krogman, a University of Pennsylvania anthropologist and an expert on the effect of fire upon the human body, said at the time. "Were I living in the Middle Ages, I'd mutter something about black magic."

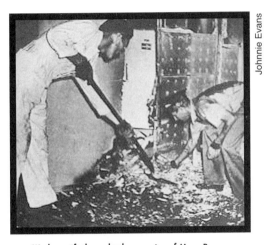

Johnnie Evans

Workers sift throught the remains of Mary Reeser

THE HOMESICK WIDOW

Back in Columbia, Pennsylvania, Mary Reeser had been the wife of the small town's foremost doctor. Her only child, Richard Jr., was in the Army Medical Corps in the St. Petersburg area during World War II and stayed there after the end of the war.

Her daughter-in-law said she always had three kinds of homemade ice cream in the freezer and was proud of her large home, good furniture, and antiques. She was always busy with needlepoint.

In 1950, three years after her husband died, she sold her

home in Pennsylvania and moved to Florida to be near her son and three small granddaughters.

But Richard Reeser Jr., said his mother soon became homesick for her old friends and miserable in the heat. She had tried without luck to rent an apartment back in Pennsylvania and had fallen into a depression.

On her last afternoon, Mary came to her son's home for Sunday dinner and babysat for her youngest granddaughter while everyone else went to the beach. With the tourists gone for the summer, it was a quiet time of year in the city. She later went home, and her son said she seemed especially despondent.

When she left her relatives, she took two Seconals on an empty stomach. She was wearing a nightgown and smoking a cigarette. Central Florida's usual summertime lightning was in the air.

Reeser's landlord and apartment neighbor, Pansy Carpenter, said she awoke to the smell of smoke about five A.M. but attributed it to a bad water pump, which she turned off before going back to sleep. When she awoke an hour later, the smell was gone.

About eight A.M., a telegram arrived from friends saying an apartment had finally turned up back in Pennsylvania. Carpenter walked it to Mary Reeser's door.

Frightened by the hot doorknob, she called to painters working nearby. They opened the door by wrapping a rag around the burning-hot knob. They looked inside.

THE SCENE

Firefighters found a thick gray haze hanging in the room. A small fire burned on an overhead wooden joist. The wall-to-wall carpeting was sticky.

Beneath Mary Reeser's body, a five-by-four-foot patch of carpeting was singed away, revealing the cement floor. The circle was so distinct that the only part of Mary Reeser's body not consumed was the foot at the end of her chronically stiff leg — found outside the circle.

Most of the apartment was untouched by fire.

Reeser's sofa bed was turned down. In one corner, the ceiling and walls from about four feet up were black with soot.

The rest of the apartment showed signs of intense heat. Electrical outlets buckled. Candles on a dresser had melted — but their wicks did not burn. A clock had stopped at 4:20 A.M. — but was undamaged and started up when plugged back in. One mirror was cracked; two were not. The refrigerator was operating. Not a single fuse had blown. The floor lamp next to the easy chair was con-

Official police photograph of Mary Reeser's charred apartment

sumed — but a pile of newspapers on a radiator five feet away was untouched.

Far off in the bathroom, a plastic tumbler had melted, but plastic toothbrushes hadn't.

The apartment had none of the odors of materials used

to start or accelerate a fire. There was no explosion.

And Mrs. Reeser's remains did not carry the sickening smell of burned human flesh.

The coroner signed the death certificate, "Accidental death by fire of unknown origin — pending further investigation."

FURTHER INVESTIGATION

Local officials called in the FBI, fire experts, and weather specialists. The death drew press and experts from around the country.

Supporters of the combustion theory had some nagging questions, many of them outlined in *Fire from Heaven, A Study of Spontaneous Combustion in Human Beings*, by British writer Michael Harrison.

Crematory experts say it takes three hours of 2,500-degree heat to cremate a body. But it would be impossible for a fire with that amount of heat to cause such limited damage. A fire that would reduce a person to cinders should have burned the apartment and everything inside.

And skulls usually explode, not shrink, in fires.

While lightning is prevalent in Tampa Bay in the summer, a stroke that hot would have blown every fuse in the apartment.

The theory that Reeser drank heavily and the large amount of alcohol in her system made her flammable was also discounted. That much alcohol would kill someone first.

And the nightgown was made of rayon acetate — a material found in nylon stockings. Touched by fire, the material flashes and makes a hole. It doesn't burst into flame.

The public contributed its own theories: suicide by paraffin or gasoline, ignition of accumulated methane in the body, murder by flame-thrower or oxygen-acetylene torch, magnesium that was then used in flashbulbs, phosphorous, and even napalm.

"A ball of fire came through the window and hit her. I seen it happen," one local resident wrote to "The Cheif of

Detectiffs."

A year after Mary Reeser's death, detective Cass Burgess said, "We still are as far from establishing any logical cause for death as we were when we first entered Mrs. Reeser's apartment."

SKEPTICS WEIGH IN

In 1984, the *Journal of the International Association of Arson Investigators* published a lengthy two-part report that found explanations for alleged combustion. And two professional sleuths provided research from a two-year investigation of 30 reported spontaneous combustion cases for stories in 1987 and 1996 in *The Skeptical Inquirer*, a newsletter that debunks the supposedly unexplained.

The two sleuths — Joe Nickell, a private detective, and Dr. John Fisher, a forensic analyst with the crime laboratory of the Orange County Sheriff's Office in Orlando — said Mary Reeser fell asleep smoking and her flammable nightie burned her up.

The Inquirer report said victims often were heavy drinkers; they would be careless with fire and unable to respond quickly. Clothes, fabric, and rugs retained melted fat flowing from bodies, feeding it back into the fire like melted wax continues to feed a candle.

In every case studied, Nickell and Fisher found a source of ignition — candles, lamps, cigarettes, fireplaces. Mary Reeser smoked.

The two found that where only some of the body was destroyed, the only fuel source was clothing. But where bodies were almost entirely consumed, sources such as chair stuffing, wooden floors, and rugs were nearby. Mary was sitting in a stuffed chair.

And they noted the fire in Mary Reeser's apartment did spread to an end table, a lamp, and a ceiling beam, and the floor was untouched because it was concrete.

They also argued the shrunken skull report resulted from second-hand accounts and was probably just a mass of muscle at the base of the skull.

Dr. Reeser never believed his mother died of spontaneous combustion. He's satisfied his mother fell asleep smoking and the fire fed on her body fat. He said his mother was five-feet-four and weighed about 175 pounds, and when she badly burned her arm once, he could see a layer of fat under her skin.

Her family insists they later felt and even smelled her perfume in their home. They said her ghost left when they finally got rid of the furniture they had salvaged from her apartment.

After months of testing, Mary Reeser's ashes were buried next to her husband's grave in Pennsylvania. She was finally home.

SOURCES

Ament, Deloris Tarzan. "Spontaneous Human Combustion: It Does Fire the Imagination," *Seattle Times*, April 1, 1990.

Harrison, Michael. *Fire from Heaven, A Study of Spontaneous Combustion in Human Beings.* New York: Methuen, 1978.

INFO, newsletter of the International Fortean Organization, Spring 1972.

Sanders, Jacquin. "Burning Death Remains Mystery," *St. Petersburg Times*, June 30, 1991.

St. Petersburg Police report on Mary Reeser's death.

UFOs OVER GULF BREEZE

What did Ed and Frances Walters see flying over their home?

The couple claims the dozens of photographs and a one-minute, 38-second video that Ed shot in a six-month span, from November 1987 to May 1988, are of spaceships over their home in Gulf Breeze.

A city council member in the Panhandle city says he, too, saw a bright orange object fly over on March 17, 1988. A retired newspaper publisher says he saw it as well. So did a doctor and a chemical engineer and his wife.

UNEARTHLY BLUE LIGHT

Ed Walters didn't just see the ships, he says. They burned his grass and shot a beam of unearthly blue light that once froze his legs to the ground and another time missed his wife by inches while he captured the encounter on film.

He reports hearing in his mind both the instructions of the aliens and discussions of earthlings he believes were being held aboard the ships. He says he saw an alien standing outside his window and by his bed.

And there's a 90-minute stretch for which he can't account that ended with him waking up face down on the beach. He believes he was a victim of an alien abduction.

In their book *The Gulf Breeze Sightings*, the Walterses call the encounters "the most astounding multiple sightings of UFOs in U.S. History."

Critics call them hoaxes.

The Walters' photographs have been described variously as double-exposure prints, the products of a faulty Polaroid, and red balloons.

"It's the wildest, most preposterous story I've ever heard," said Philip J. Klass, a senior editor of *Aviation Week & Space Technology* magazine for 34 years, who has been exposing and explaining UFO hoaxes and reports since 1966 and publishes the *UFO Skeptics Newsletters*.

"Just think of it," Klass said in 1990. "Multiple visits to the same house, little creatures, voices in his head."

Walters, a building contractor by profession, got an advance for his book — one report said $200,000. Walters says it was "a lot less than that," and that he probably lost money in the process because his business dried up.

"What we did was think that by writing it down, it would stop people like you from calling," Frances Walters laughed in a 1996 telephone interview. "How wrong we were."

In the book, experts from both the U.S. Navy and Polaroid attest to the authenticity of the pictures. A polygraph test showed Walters believes what he says.

In the years since he went public with his encounters, Walters says, he has averaged 100 to 150 letters a week and 10 to 15 calls a day — not from critics or supporters, but mostly from people who also claim encounters.

"When you describe yourself as a UFO witness, you tend not to be skeptical of someone else's UFO story," he said. He does say none of the thousands who have contacted him report being deliberately hurt in any way.

In June 1990, the *Pensacola News Journal* said it had discovered a model in the Walters' former home and took photographs of it similar to those Walters presented to the world.

Walters later presented evidence that showed the model couldn't have been involved in his photos and didn't match them and said he would never be stupid enough to leave a hoax's smoking gun for someone to find. He said it was probably planted during the 10 months the home was empty before being sold, probably by someone out to debunk him.

A FACE IN THE WINDOW

Walters' first encounter came on Veteran's Day 1987.

His wife and teenaged daughter were out, and his son was in the recreation room, blasting the big-screen television.

Walters was in his yard when he saw the glowing, blue-gray ship. He rushed inside for his Polaroid. Outside again, a blue beam struck him and grabbed him like a vise. He couldn't move. He couldn't yell. He couldn't breathe.

A voice in his head said, "We will not harm you."

He was lifted two feet into the air. Just as suddenly, the beam went off like a light, and he fell to the ground, gasping and gagging and reeking of a combination of cinnamon and ammonia.

Six days later, pretending to represent an anonymous associate, he turned in five photos to the weekly *Gulf Breeze Sentinel*. Two of them were published two days after that on the front page, with an unsigned letter describing the encounter.

NOVEMBER 20: Walters' head was filled with a maddening hum; he then heard an unknown language in his head. He saw a light falling swiftly in the sky. A voice in his mind said, "Be calm. Step forward." When he began taking photographs, it said, "Don't do that." Another, in Spanish — which he learned during six years in Costa Rica — said, "Los fotos son prohibido": photos prohibited.

A voice said the aliens had the right to take Walters. It said they would be back. Then the ship shot off.

He had shot photos six through nine and decided it was time to load his shotgun and pistol.

NOVEMBER 25: By now, others were writing and calling the *Gulf Breeze Sentinel* to report sightings. They included

Ed Walters

The Walterses say this blue beam just missed Frances

several motorists and a Florida Highway Patrol trooper who pulled off in nearby Navarre about two A.M. to watch a strange light. The trooper's photographs were published in another paper. Military and civilian air traffic controllers reported no unusual aircraft.

Representatives of Mutual UFO Network (MUFON) arrived as well. And the local and national media were beginning to talk about the spaceships.

<u>DECEMBER 2</u>: Ed awakened in the dead of night to the sounds of a baby crying and people speaking in Spanish. He presumed the computerlike voice he heard was that of the aliens.

He stepped onto the patio and saw a ship drop from the heavens. He snapped photo 10. The ship shot away.

A short time later, something woke him again. Pulling back his blind, he suddenly saw a creature through the window. It was four feet tall with big black eyes, dressed in a box-shaped outfit and holding a glowing silver rod. Walters screamed and stumbled backward.

As the creature walked away, Walters chased it across his patio. Suddenly the blue beam seized him. He somehow pulled his foot away and got photo 11 — the ship's blue beam lifting its crew member from a nearby field.

DECEMBER 3: *The Sentinel* published two photos taken a year earlier by another resident. Other residents were also writing in to report sightings.

DECEMBER 5: About 5:30 A.M., Walters saw a different, much larger craft and shot photo 12. The voices again called for him.

DECEMBER 10: A couple from a town 85 miles north, just across the Alabama line, reported the same ship and blue beam. And two friends saw a craft over the Pensacola Bay Bridge.

DECEMBER 17: Walters awoke to find several figures standing by his bed. He followed them outside and saw a ship 150 feet up. Standing in boxer shorts, he shot photo 13. The ship dropped smoke and liquid onto the ground. He saw the ship again but it was bigger. He shot photos 15, 16, and 17.

DECEMBER 22: "Believer Bill," a neighbor two blocks away, shot nine photos of three craft.

DECEMBER 23: At six A.M., Walters saw three craft together and snapped photo 18.

DECEMBER 24: *The Sentinel* published *Bill's* photos.

DECEMBER 27: A college friend of the Walters' son was at the house and also saw the ship.

DECEMBER 28: Walters shot a one-minute, 38-second video of the craft.

JANUARY 12, 1988: A beam intercepted Walters' truck as he headed to a job site. Partially paralyzed, he got the truck off the road and grabbed his camera, shooting photo 19. Blue beams deposited five creatures. They began walking toward him. He slammed his truck into reverse and fled.

JANUARY 13: Two men saying they were from Air Force Special Security Services and waving something called a

Ed Walters

One of Ed Walters' controversial photographs

"materials seizure warrant" demanded Walters' UFO photos.

JANUARY 16: Walters saw two ships and shot photo 20.

JANUARY 17: Walters met with MUFON's national director, Walter Andrus, who had arrived from Texas. His group now had six investigators in Gulf Breeze.

JANUARY 18: MUFON investigators began surveillance.

JANUARY 21: Walters saw a ship, but a MUFON investigator, distracted by what turned out to be a plane, missed it.

JANUARY 22: A mysterious military helicopter circled the Walters' house. The family began to fear the government was watching. Another resident filed a sighting report with *The Sentinel*.

JANUARY 24: Walters shot photo 21; the editor of *The Sentinel* videotaped Walters' nervous system reacting to the alien voices.

JANUARY 25: A 10-foot spot of dried-out grass was discovered.

JANUARY 26: Walters, called out of the shower by his wife and clad only in a towel, confronted a ship hovering over his patio. It flew off. Frances Walters shot the stand-off between her husband and the spacecraft — photos 22 and 23.

FEBRUARY 7: Walters shot photo 24, of Frances barely dodging a blue beam on the patio.

February 18: Walters took a polygraph test that concluded he believes what he said he saw. *The Sentinel* published more sighting reports.

FEBRUARY 19: A man told the newspaper the UFOs had threatened to blow up the town unless *The Sentinel* ran his story.

FEBRUARY 26: Walters shot a spacecraft — photos 25–34 — with a special four-lens camera supplied by MUFON. It shot four frames at once, providing more detail and assuring four negatives for inspection.

MARCH 3: Still more sightings appeared in *The Sentinel*.

MARCH 8: In his seventeenth sighting, Walters shot photo 35 of a ship in the distance.

MARCH 17: The Walterses and others spotted a craft; Walters shot it with a special double-image stereo camera.

MARCH 20: Walters stepped outside his home and shot two photos — 37L and 37R.

APRIL 20: Walters recounted three episodes in his life, about eight years apart, when he couldn't account for time. He wondered whether he had been abducted.

Ed Walters' twentieth and final encounter came May 1, 1988, fully six months after the first sighting, at a waterfront park.

He shot photos 38L and 38R. Just after shooting photo 39, he saw a white flash. The next thing he remembers is lifting his face and chest off the wet sand. An hour and 15 minutes had passed. His head throbbed. Black material under the fingernails of his right hand reeked of a mysterious odor that would not go away. He discovered a bruise on the back of his head, another on the bridge of his nose and one at each temple; all of them had a red dot in the middle.

". . . WHATEVER THEY MIGHT BE."
In 1994, the Walterses published *UFO Abductions in Gulf Breeze*. It's based on Walters' recollections, under hypnosis, of the three earlier episodes in which he says he might have been abducted. The Walterses gave graphic details of encounters in those three incidents but can't swear they actually happened.

"The mind is a very complicated machine, if you will, and you have to be very careful that the hypnosis is truly giving memories that are not polluted by other memories," Ed Walters said.

Walters still can't explain why his personal ordeal stopped at the end of that six-month stretch in 1987 and 1988.

"Often, there are questions that can only be answered by the beings responsible for the UFOs, whatever they might be," he said. "I can't answer what they're thinking or what they're doing or what their agenda is. I tend to think it's beyond our understanding. It's not something that's within our grasp to even understand."

SOURCES

Associated Press. "Photographer's UFO May be Model in Attic," *Palm Beach Post*, June 11, 1990.

Hayes, Ron. "Close Encounters," *Palm Beach Post*, May 10, 1993.

Hiaasen, Rob. "The Objects of Their Attention," *Palm Beach Post*, May 19, 1990.

Interview with Ed Walters, July 12, 1996.

Lavin, Chris. "Debunkers vs. Believers," *St. Petersburg Times*, July 8, 1990.

Walters, Ed and Frances. *The Gulf Breeze Sightings*. New York: William Morrow and Company, 1990.

Walters, Ed and Frances. *UFO Abductions in Gulf Breeze*. New

York: William Morrow and Company, 1994.

Walters, Ed, and Bruce MacCabee. *UFOs Are Real: Here's the Proof.* New York: Avon, 1997.

OTHER SIGHTINGS

LANTANA, AUGUST 1952:
Boy Scout scoutmaster Sonny DesVergers emerged burned and dazed from a wooded area, claiming he had encountered an alien spacecraft that zapped him with a fireball fired from a domed hatch. "I heard hinges open and then they shot at me," DesVergers told the local newspaper. Decades later, two of his former scouts backed DesVergers' story. And Lymon Bradford, who lived a few miles away in suburban West Palm Beach, said years later that an object landed in the back of his family's property that same night. He said air force investigators later confiscated pictures of the object his father took.

Palm Beach Post, July 13, 1997

SOLONA, JULY 1972:
Two families reported seeing an object that looked like a bright yellow lightbulb falling and trailing smoke. One man said he saw it above his car, and it seemed to follow him to his driveway; he was afraid to get out for 90 minutes before it finally left. The families said the object was there for several days, and they were afraid it was watching them.

Punta Gorda Daily Herald-News, July 15, 1972

WINTER HAVEN, JANUARY 1979:
A police officer said he saw a UFO flying over Polk County Community College. He described it as a large, round, orange-yellow ball and said he and another officer tried to chase it, but it got away.

Fort Lauderdale Sun-Sentinel, July 12, 1987

OCALA NATIONAL FOREST, JUNE 1987:
An Ocala woman said a mysterious metallic craft landed in her front yard. Five people in Citra said a large, silent object hovered near power lines just above their car. Several campers and motorists near the forest reported objects, and others made anonymous calls to authorities. And a deputy said he saw a flying craft that made no noise, was shaped like no aircraft he'd ever seen, and moved "at an extraordinarily high rate of speed."

St. Petersburg Times, July 9, 1987

FORT LAUDERDALE, NOVEMBER 1991:
A woman reported seeing a massive boomerang-shaped spaceship "two stories high and big as two blocks of streets."

Palm Beach Post, May 10, 1993

HERNANDO COUNTY, APRIL 1993:
At least nine coastal residents and a sheriff's deputy reported seeing a boomerang-shaped object with a wingspan of at least 200 feet.

St. Petersburg Times, April 21, 1993

MIAMI-DADE COUNTY, WINTER 1996–97:
A gym teacher and 13 students on a Miami-Edison High School ball field saw a round object climb into the sky and disappear. A couple videotaped and three other witnesses observed a "pink fuzzy hamburger" shape over Homestead. Coral Gables residents saw an object flicker, plummet, and zigzag away. Three people sailing near Key Largo saw a circling white object; their compasses went haywire. A Perrine woman saw five lights in a domino pattern glide overhead, then soar off in a flash of red.

Fort Lauderdale Sun-Sentinel, March 9, 1997

THE KORESHAN

Stand on the promenade. Feel the shells crunch underfoot on the path. Tune out the traffic on U.S. 41, just a few yards away, and listen carefully for the sounds of the marching band, its music bouncing off the trees that line the Estero River in Estero, about 15 miles south of Fort Myers.

See the wood-and-concrete Founder's Home, restored to its turn-of-the-century splendor — when it was, for millions, the nucleus of a New Jerusalem that would be carved out of the swamps of Southwest Florida.

Look to the porch for the charismatic leader — a pied piper who based a religion on his belief that we live not on top of the Earth, but inside it, and who established a church on the foundations of communal living and pureness of body and mind.

The vision died soon after the man, even though the faithful waited in vain in the hot sun for his corpse to rise and lead them to a new world order.

Now the old buildings, the meandering river, and the tall trees of the Koreshan (pronounced kuh-RESH-in) State Historic Site are all that remain of this New Jerusalem.

Each fall, the Koreshan Solar Festival, believed to be one of Florida's oldest continuously observed celebrations, celebrates Dr. Cyrus Reed Teed, founder of the Koreshan.

Members of the Koreshan community

"People said he was crazy, but look how many followed him; he had to be very dynamic," says Brad Burris, a ranger at the 100-acre site, part of 305 acres given by Teed's followers to the state in 1961. Ironically, the donation by the followers, who imagined a city for millions, has kept the site from joining the sprawl that has changed Southwest Florida.

"If it weren't for that [the donation], you'd have condominiums on the Estero River; you better believe it," says Sue Roper, public relations director for Koreshan Unity Inc., the only remaining fragment of the Koreshans.

The corporation occupies a round building with glass walls and a view of a thick forest across U.S. 41 from the historic site.

Inside, hundreds of tattered books from the original Koreshan community line shelves along with Koreshan brochures, photographs, and other materials.

The corporation continues to operate, pressing for intelligent use of natural resources — a popular idea now but in many ways as bizarre a concept a century ago as the other ones put forth by the Koreshans.

The group's mission is not to spread the religion but to be its historian, President Jo Bigelow says. She stresses that, despite its offbeat vision of the universe, the group espouses some modern tenets.

"They had no prejudices," Bigelow said. "They were ahead of their time."

On the wall hangs a giant piece of concrete that reads, "Cyrus Shepherd, Stone of Israel." It's all that remains of the tomb of Cyrus Teed.

THE SEVENTH MESSENGER

Cyrus Teed came a century before another Koresh — David — would draw the world's attention to Waco, Texas. There, an April 19, 1993, FBI assault on the Branch Davidian cult compound led to a fire and the death of 86 cult members.

Born in 1839 to a Baptist family in upstate New York, Teed became a brain surgeon and came to question accepted concepts of the universe's structure.

In 1870, as he meditated in his lab, he was visited by an angel in a gown of purple and gold with "long, golden tresses of profusely luxuriant growth over her shoulders."

The angel, Teed said, gave him a "divine revelation": The universe did not surround but instead was completely enclosed by the Earth — a hollow "macroscopic egg" about 8,000 miles in diameter. The Earth's surface lies along the inside lining, and the moon, planets, and stars all revolve around the sun, an electromagnetic battery at the center of it all.

Twenty-eight years later, at Naples Beach, Teed would spread a giant wood-and-brass device along the water's edge, point it toward the horizon, and perform an experiment he claimed proved that the Earth's surface was concave. He would brazenly offer $10,000 to anyone who could refute his conclusions; there would be no takers.

Koreshan Unity, Inc.

Cyrus Reed Teed founded the Koreshan

Shortly after his visit from the angel, Teed founded the Koreshanity in Chicago.

He preached that when the sexes blended into one eternal and noble entity, world perfection would be attained. He said the flesh is immortal through reincarnation.

He disdained profanity, tobacco, and liquor and said his Utopia would allow "no bawdy houses, no tobacco shops, no distilleries, no breweries, no gambling houses nor other forms or dens of vice."

He embraced ecology, racial and sexual tolerance, celibacy, communal living, and communal ownership of all property.

He proclaimed himself the prophet "Koresh," Hebrew for Cyrus and for shepherd, and the "seventh messenger — the prophet who would usher in the millennium." He predicted Koreshanity would become one of the world's great religions.

REFUGE

Teed's founding group met opposition in upstate New York and other settlements across the nation. He was constantly threatened, and groups reportedly gathered to plot his lynching. Teed eventually met a Fort Myers businessman who suggested he and his group might find refuge and peace of mind in Southwest Florida.

Teed came to the area, where a German-born farmer and widower became so enthralled he promptly joined up and donated his land along the banks of the Estero.

"People coming to us in Estero come to a pioneer life, one of strenuosity and sacrifice," Teed wrote. Some 200 of his 4,000 devotees came. Battling the heat and mosquitoes, they planned and began building what he said would grow into a sprawling metropolis.

"It will contain 10 million people, white and black, and will become the greatest city in the world," Teed wrote.

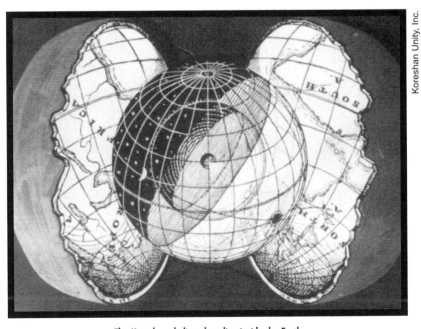

Koreshan Unity, Inc.

The Koreshans believed we live inside the Earth

Forests were cleared and lush gardens planted. Maps were drawn showing 600-foot-wide roads emanating from a hub at Teed's headquarters. Waste would travel on a conveyer to a location 50 miles away. "There will be no dumping of the public waste into the rivers, bays, and gulfs."

Buildings and halls were planned. A marching band, an orchestra, pageants, and plays were organized.

"Koreshanity defends faith of the Jew in the Old Testament and of the Christian in both Old and New Testaments," reads a hand-painted sign, one of several original Koreshan objects gathering dust on the stage of the Art Hall — one of eight buildings still standing out of the original 60.

In the hall, you can find the original instruments of the orchestra. And on a giant table stands a model showing a globe split in half like an eggshell to show the continents lining its inner surface and, at its center, the sun, with stars swirling around it.

On one wall, an oil painting portrays the New Jerusalem. On it appears the Latin phrase *vincit qoi se vincet* — he conquers who conquers himself.

Teed's followers established the area's first school and numerous businesses — including a 200-loaf-a-day bakery, a general store, a boatyard, a machine shop, and agricultural processing centers. They built a publishing house, where they produced their newspaper, *The American Eagle*. It is still published today by Koreshan Unity.

WAITING FOR TEED

At its peak, about 250 people populated "New Jerusalem," which had spread across 7,500 acres of Lee County and other sites across America. It was welcomed by many southwestern Floridians. But some people in nearby Fort Myers did not care for its residents' liberal views on racial and sexual equality and feared their voting power.

One day, as Teed waited to pick up a Koreshanity member at the Fort Myers train station, a local resident began berating him and roughing him up. A sheriff's deputy came upon the scuffle, struck Teed in the head, and carted him off to jail for disturbing the peace. Charges were later dropped, and two years later, on December 22, 1908, Teed died at the age of 69. Followers said they believed the beating had hastened his death.

Because of their trust in reincarnation, Teed's followers laid his body on a plank on Estero Island and waited patiently for him to return to life. After four days, the remains showed no signs of movement. Finally, the health inspector insisted Teed be interred. Devastated devotees laid Teed in a four-by-eight-foot, five-foot-tall tomb.

Twelve years later, a hurricane swept the tomb away. All that was left was Teed's tombstone, an act that stirred the faith of the Koreshans.

But politics and infighting took their toll on the group. A Tennessee factory, whose mortgage had been guaranteed by the Koreshans, failed, causing financial stress on the group. Finally, a large section split off, and many of those who remained succumbed to old age. By 1940, the Koreshans had dwindled in number to 36 and had an average age of 79.

New life was breathed into the Koreshans with the arrival in 1940 of Hedwig Michael. The Jewish-born immigrant who fled Nazi persecution turned her life over to Koreshanity and its teachings, becoming the group's leader and only acknowledged member after the last three original Koreshans died in the 1960s.

Michael is responsible for the deeding of the site "as a gift to the people." She died at the age of 90 in August 1982 and is buried next to the bakery.

"Be ashamed to die until you have won some victory for humanity," reads her grave marker. Around it, the grounds of the park have been restored to look as they did during Koreshanity's "golden years" — 1904 to 1907.

"When I first moved here, I thought they were a bunch of kooks," Koreshan's Sue Roper says of the group. "I could-

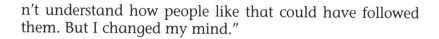

n't understand how people like that could have followed them. But I changed my mind."

The Koreshan State Historic Site is south of Fort Myers. Take Interstate 75 to Exit 19, to Corkscrew Road, west two miles to U.S. 41. Admission charged. Write to Box 7, Estero, FL 33928. Call (941) 992-0311.

The Koreshan Unity Foundation, Inc., Box 97, Estero , FL 33928. Call (941) 992-2184.

SOURCES

Bickel, Karl A. *The Mangrove Coast: The Story of the West Coast of Florida.* Omni Print Media, 1989.

Damkohler, Elwin E. *Memoirs of the First Settler.* Fort Myers, Fla.: Island Press, 1967.

Kleinberg, Howard. "Waco's David Koresh had a Predecessor in Old Florida," *Miami Herald*, April 6, 1993.

McIver, Stuart. "Take Exit 19 to the Promised Land," *Sunshine Magazine, Fort Lauderdale Sun-Sentinel*, October 22, 1989.

Teed, Cyrus Reed. *The Cellular Cosmogony.* Estero, Fla.: Guiding Star Publishing House, 1905.

CASSADAGA

Cassadaga is a "company" town 25 miles southwest of Daytona Beach. Several of the 350 residents are in the same business: they are psychics, mediums, and spiritual healers.

Founded in 1875, the town — listed on the National Register of Historic Places as a historic district — is tucked away in a hilly patch of pine and palmetto next to Spirit Pond, a lake shaped like an hourglass.

The place has no traffic light or even a gas pump. But some 50,000 people visit it every year and more than 1,000 will come in a single weekend.

There are 50 certified mediums at the Cassadaga Camp; about half actually do readings. Another 20 or so "freelance" psychic readers live outside the camp.

In 1875, medium George Colby came to North Florida from upstate New York. He claimed to follow three spirits: Philosopher, a German entity; Wanda, who channeled healing; and a Professor Huffman, who worked with Colby when he presented public messages.

Colby wanted to, and did, establish a winter home for spiritualists. Several early mediums came from Cassadaga, a small settlement near Lily Dale, New York – "the fountainhead of modern spiritualism." *Cassadaga* is Seneca Indian for "rocks beneath the water."

"All ordained spiritualist ministers may use the title of 'reverend,' give spiritual advice and messages and fulfill the duties and powers belonging to the pastorage of a recognized church," say the camp rules, as reported in the 1930s classic *WPA Guide to Florida*. "Certified mediums may exercise any and all phases of mediumship, trance, clairvoyance, clairaudience, trumpet, healing, etc., but not the duties of a pastor. The local board of directors shall specify the qualifications of their ministers, mediums, lecturers and healers, and shall duly certify the same when found satisfactory."

The Southern Cassadaga Spiritualist Camp Meeting Association, incorporated in 1894, claims to be the oldest active religious community in the Southeast. It owns about 57 acres of land in the heart of the settlement; the site includes a church, a meeting hall, and houses built by members who live and work there.

Don't call them fortune-tellers.

"It implies a preset destiny," says Barbara Joy Hines-Bengtson, president of the association. "We believe in free will and personal responsibility. We also believe life is eternal. Every action you take can have an effect or influence on what may be laid out."

And they don't take kindly to ridicule, Hines-Bengtson says. "We recognize that this is our life. It's science, it's philosophy, and it's religion, just as a Catholic would be offended if someone came in and started carrying on about all their beliefs," she says.

"Spiritualism is not a proselytizing religion. They'll find their way to us and we'll be ready in service — not on the corner waving signs."

Cassadaga is near Lake Helen in Volusia County. Take Interstate 4 to Exit 54, turn right on County Road 4101, then right again on County Road 4139. Write Box 319, Cassadaga, FL 32706. Call (904) 228-2880.

SOURCES

Associated Press/*Palm Beach Post*, December 29, 1988.

Henderson, Jamie. *The Story of Cassadaga*. Cassadaga, Fla.: Reverend Jamie Henderson, 1992.

Interview with Barbara Joy Hines-Bengtson, President, Southern Cassadaga Spiritualist Camp Meeting Association, December 10, 1997.

Interview with journalist and Cassadaga specialist Patrick McCallister, December 9, 1997.

Wall Street Journal/Palm Beach Post, March 31, 1990.

CORAL CASTLE

Hurricane Andrew's 1992 attack on southern Miami-Dade County only increased the mystery of Coral Castle.

While the storm tore apart homes and buildings across the region and collapsed the roof of the attraction's gift shop, Edward Leedskalnin's baffling legacy was unscathed.

If winds estimated at up to 200 miles per hour couldn't budge the 1,100 tons of Florida coral — in pieces ranging in size from six to 30 tons — how did a five-foot, 100-pound man lift and position them? Seven decades after his feat, no one has come up with answers.

Leedskalnin isn't saying. The Latvian immigrant worked in obscurity for three decades and died the same way in 1951. The attraction was placed on the National Register of Historic Places in 1984.

His published works exalt various scientific laws, Florida, the family, and a lost love. He wrote five books with such titles as *Magnetic Base* and *Cosmic Force*.

Leedskalnin carved and sculpted using only handmade pulleys and levers salvaged from car and railroad junk-yards. He claimed he employed the long-lost secrets of the pyramids.

Coral Castle's sculptures were carved from tons of coral

Among his creations are:

✗ A nine-ton gate that swings open with the touch of a finger.

✗ A table in the shape of Florida; the geographically correct, eight-inch indentation representing Lake Okeechobee is kept filled with water.

✗ A 20-ton, 20-foot-tall telescope with a circular cutout that constantly points to the North Star.

✗ A sundial that tells time and indicates equinox and solstice days.

✗ The "throne room," a collection of several chairs. In one chair, called "the mad rocker," two people sit facing each other and rock. Another, called "the mother-in-law," is identified as the most uncomfortable chair.

✗ "The world's largest valentine," a two-and-a-half-ton heart-shaped table with benches, is said to honor the fiancée who jilted Leedskalnin back in Latvia around 1915. Deciding the 27-year-old man was too old for her, the 16-year-old girl broke up with him the night they were to marry. Heartbroken, he roamed through

Canada, Washington, and California before ending up in Florida City, in what was then the frontier of sparsely populated South Florida.

Leedskalnin opened his attraction to the public in 1923 as "Ed's Place." It's mentioned in the 1939 *WPA Guide to Florida*. That year, opting for greater visibility along U.S. 1 and for fortune that was never to materialize, Leedskalnin moved his entire inventory to its present location.

Borrowing a mule and a wagon, Leedskalnin hauled the colossal carvings 10 miles and set them in place. Again, no one knows how he did it.

An author and commercial airline pilot from New Zealand credits "a vast power grid that governs a whole array of extraordinary and unrelated world phenomena . . . set up between some groups on this planet and the UFOs."

The pilot suggests the castle is at the perfect intersection of such grids; providing "the geometric harmonies necessary for the manipulation of antigravity."

Coral Castle is on U.S. 1 at S.W. 286th Street, just north of Homestead. Take Florida's Turnpike about 25 miles south of Miami to S.W. 137 Avenue; go south to S.W. 288 Street (Biscayne Drive); west to S.W. 157 Avenue; then north about a block to U.S. 1. Continuous self-guided tours every day, 9 A.M. to 5 P.M. Call (305) 248-6344.

THE BARDIN BOOGER

Randy Medlock says he saw the Bardin Booger.

"That was my original story, and I won't back down from anybody, because I did see it," Medlock said.

The thing was big, he said. And hairy. And it looked like a bear with a pug nose but walked more like a man.

The six-foot, four-inch Medlock said his size-13 feet were lost in the thing's footprints, and he was unable to stretch his frame to fit both feet in the two indentations.

Only Medlock and a handful of other Bardin residents say they've seen the hairy beast, a kind of Southern cousin to Bigfoot, in this community of about 1,500 people just northwest of Palatka. It seems the Booger has gone the way of the Loch Ness monster, UFOs, and Elvis in the produce aisle.

But that doesn't mean he's been forgotten. There are reminders all around, such as the five-dollar "Booger Burger" offered by one restaurant, or the profits local businesses make on Booger hats, cups, pins, and T-shirts. A song has even been recorded about the hairy creature.

If you believe the T-shirts and caps, the Booger is a large, muscular thing with a long, red tongue.

It is said to have a less-than-pleasant aroma, although how anyone got close enough to catch a whiff of it is not clear.

Medlock, who had initially kept quiet for fear no one would believe him, was miffed when a tabloid embellished his story by saying the monster tore up a dog pen and ate one of Medlock's hounds.

Published reports about the Booger have put the tiny town of Bardin on the map. However, tales of the beast roaming the backwoods were around long before Mayor Bud Key set up a convenience store in Bardin where he sells Booger T-shirts and hats.

Some believe the Booger is an escaped gorilla. But Key said no circus ever came through the area.

Billy Crain portrays the Bardin Booger

Some stories blame locals who dress up and scare a few farmers or hunters, thus perpetuating the legend.

And you will find a costumed "Booger Jr.," growling and stamping at store openings and radio station remotes in Palatka.

Inside the homemade Booger suit is either Billy Crain or his wife. Besides the personal appearances, Crain has also made a few Booger-bucks selling T-shirts, pins, and dolls or crooning the song he's written. Recorded in 1981, Crain claims he's sold about 2,000 copies:

Hey Mr. Bardin Booger,
Bardin is your home,
and every day you love to roam.
You run through the bushes
and you run through the trees.
Hey Mr. Bardin Booger,
don't get me, please!

If the creature emerged, Crain isn't above offering a cut of the profits he's made over the years. He says he's gone on many a horseback "Booger hunt" but hasn't seen the creature yet.

"Some of the old-timers will swear by the thing," Crain said. "I don't say yay or nay. That'd spoil all the fun."

But he said, "How could it live that long in legend if there weren't something to it?"

Other sightings of similar beasts that might have been the Booger or its kin:

✗ NOVEMBER 1966, BROOKSVILLE:
A woman claimed she had stopped to change a flat tire and, encountering a nauseating odor, looked up to see a large, hairy creature shaped like a man but with the face of an ape walking toward her. She said the monster sat and watched her until another car passed; the beast then grunted and walked off. Less than eight months later, a trucker reported he was driving on Interstate 75 in the same area when he pulled off to doze. He said an ape-man appeared at his open door and tried to drag him out. He said he wrestled and struck the reeking animal, which was holding him under its arm. It finally dropped him, then chased him back to his truck. His air horn scared it off.

✗ NOVEMBER 1977, MARION COUNTY:
A hunter reported seeing an "apelike creature," eight

feet tall and weighing about 800 pounds. The hunter fired his gun six times but apparently missed. Three miles away, a Baptist minister cutting wood in Ocala National Forest was confronted by an eight-foot-tall creature covered in black hair.

CREATURES FROM THE SEA

✗ THE ST. AUGUSTINE LUMP:
In November 1896, on St. Augustine Beach, a four- to five-ton lump of pink organic matter washed ashore. It was described as 23 feet long, four feet high, and 18 feet across the widest part of its back. The arms were 75 to 100 feet long and 18 inches in diameter at their base. A doctor declared the remains those of an octopus. In 1971 scientists examined preserved tissue from the Smithsonian Institution and agreed.

✗ CHARLEY THOMPSON'S MONSTER:
When tourists boating on Biscayne Bay in 1908 said they saw a sea serpent "with long fins just back of the head," "a body at least 30 feet in length" and a "long

Miami News

Charley Thompson and his big fish

slender neck," famed Miami fisherman Charley Thompson went in pursuit. He never found it, but four years later, on June 1, 1912, in the part of the Keys where the 7-Mile-Bridge now stands, he hooked into a giant fish. Thirty-nine hours, five harpoons, and 151 bullets later, he landed the 15-ton whale shark. A tug towed it the 110 miles back to Miami. He promptly stuffed it and began touring the country with it. Of course, we know about fish after three days — this behemoth soon stank so badly that the tour ended.

✗ THE INDIAN RIVER MONSTER:

At least three people reported seeing the beast between 1982 and 1987 in Brevard County waters. One said, "I was drift fishing off Cove Three north of the Pineda Causeway. Drifting backward, I turned and there it was about 100 feet ahead of me, watching me intently. A long, slender neck and head, something like a dinosaur head. About four feet high. Throat was light yellow, head grayish green. At about 50 feet, it slowly submerged. Seemed friendly and not at all afraid of me."

SOURCES

Florida Living, July 1993.

INFO, newsletter of the International Fortean Organization, May, July 1976.

Kleinberg, Howard. *The Way We Were*. Miami: Surfside Press, 1985.

Ocala Star Banner, November 19, 1977.

Orlando Sentinel, November 19, 1987.

Punta Gorda Daily Herald News, June 28, 1976.

Wildstein, Karen. "The Tale of the River Dragon," *Florida Today*, February 12, 1987.

SPOOK HILL

Pull up to the sign. Read the legend. Move up to the line. Stop. Put the car in neutral. Come off the brake.

It. Ever. So. Slowly. Begins. Rolling. Up. Hill.

Before you know it, you've rolled backward about 500 feet, on past the sign, and you're scratching your head, and so are the kids.

Okay, here's the secret:

Because Spook Hill is surrounded by rolling hills, the whole horizon is at a cockeyed angle and your perspective is thrown off. Take the hills away and you can tell you've just rolled down.

Although Lake Wales does get plenty of mileage out of Spook Hill, the town — to its credit — never went the next step of blocking off the road, charging admission, and routing the only way out of the neighborhood through a gift shop. It may well be the last free tourist attraction in Central Florida.

The story goes that circuit riders traversing the area and, later, citrus workers hauling their wagons around the lake, noticed their horses appeared to be laboring downhill. When the road was paved and cars began suffering the same fate, Spook Hill was born.

The hill is in a residential neighborhood at the north

Do cars go uphill at Spook Hill?

end of the town, just north of State Road 60 and just east of U.S. 27.

It's right on the way for many tourists hitting the nearby Bok Tower, on their way to Cypress Gardens, or taking a short cut to Disney World.

There's not much to the place, just a couple of lines painted on the road and a billboard bearing the figure of a cartoon ghost and describing this Indian legend:

A Seminole chief and his people had settled in the area. A giant bull alligator took up residence in an adjacent lake, then began raiding the village.

Seeing his people terrified, the powerful and courageous chief, placed under the protection of the Great Spirit by the tribe's shaman and elders, set out after the animal.

It took many days before he came across the alligator, dragging another night's victim into the lake. The chief and the beast struggled for a month; finally the thrashing stopped and the water turned red. As his subjects watched in terror and anticipation to see if either combatant would emerge from the lake, the chief rose from the water triumphant.

The hill is said to be haunted by the alligator seeking revenge or the great chief trying to protect his people from the encroachment of the white man.

The folks at Spook Hill Elementary School, adjacent to the road, say there's a steady stream of motorists and that the illusion was even more dramatic before homes were built across the hillside.

Spook Hill is in Lake Wales. Take State Road 60 west to Alternate U.S. 27; north past Central Avenue, then east at the first traffic light (North Avenue). Then turn left on the one-way street to Spook Hill. No admission charged.

Lake Wales Area Chamber of Commerce: Box 191, Lake Wales, FL 33859-0191. Call (941) 676-3445.

Polk County Tourist Development Council: (800) 828-7655.

THE BAT TOWER

Perhaps only in the Florida Keys can you find a 30-foot monument to bat droppings.

The infamous Bat Tower, on a little key about 13 miles north of Key West, is the definitive "it seemed like a good idea at the time."

Henry Flagler's railroad had opened up the Keys, previously a string of unconnected islands accessible only by boat. The tourists would not be far behind. Perhaps they could deal with the lack of air-conditioning. But no one would last long under the onslaught of South Florida's flying vampire — the mosquito.

Richter Clyde Perky, one of a flood of speculators, saw booming 1920s South Florida as a land of milk and honey. In 1929, he came from Colorado and bought 25,000 acres on Sugarloaf Key. Using the legendary, tough Dade County pine, he built a tower 12 feet off the ground on stilts. He posted a plaque at the base saying the tower was "dedicated to good health at Perky, Florida."

Then Perky waited. He was waiting for . . . bats.

Perky figured the tower would attract the winged mammals, known to frequent the lower Keys; they would then feast on the mosquitoes, ridding the area of its biggest tourism impediment.

The Bat Tower never attracted bats.

Andy Newman, Florida Keys Tourist Development Council

Perky learned a single bat could eat 3,000 mosquitoes and figured the tower could house 100,000 bats.

But like everyone in South Florida's boom, his motives were not limited to the altruistic.

The tower had a big chute down its center. Bags at the bottom would collect what the bats produced — considered the finest, and most expensive, fertilizer.

Hearing of a successful bat fertilizer venture in Texas, Perky sent away for the building plans and a box costing $500, which was filled with a secret bat bait said to be made of bat guano and ground female bat sex organs.

The smell was said to keep people away for days. Bats stayed away, too. And a hurricane blew away the bait box. One story, discounted by many, says Perky brought in nearly 1,000 bats, which promptly flew off. But Fred Johnson, who built the tower for Perky, told a reporter in 1987 that just wasn't true.

Perky, victim of an apparent con to the tune of $10,000, died in 1941 at 62 and is buried in Miami. Now his tower is on the National Register of Historic Places, and truck- and plane-delivered pesticides help control the insects, although any visitor or resident knows it is a battle that will never be won.

Residents say the tower has never attracted bats, only curious visitors who stare at the tower, pausing now and then to slap their necks.

The Bat Tower is on the property of the Sugarloaf Lodge resort, on the north (Florida Bay) side of U.S. 1 at Mile Marker 17. The tower cannot be entered but can be viewed for free. Write Sugarloaf Lodge, Box 148-S, Sugarloaf Key, FL 33044. Call (305) 745-3211.

SOURCES

Klingener, Nancy. "Batty Idea to fight mosquitoes gains credence in Keys," *Miami Herald*, March 9, 1997.

Pancake, John. "A Keys Quirk: The Bat Tower," *Miami Herald*, January 2, 1985.

Sutton, Jane. "No Bats in the Belfry," United Press International, *Fort Lauderdale Sun-Sentinel*, October 4, 1987.

THE SNAKE MAN

Bill Haast waved a scarred hand inches from a king cobra, the world's deadliest animal. Distracting it, he reached with the other hand to grab it around what passes for a neck on the nearly 14-foot snake.

Suddenly, the cobra, a reptile that can kill an elephant with a single bite, lunged with the swiftness of a cracking whip. It barely missed sinking its fangs into Haast's hand and releasing enough venom to kill 100 people. Then Haast had the snake and was forcing its fangs onto a membrane-covered test tube.

Haast has repeated that process many times with the world's most poisonous species of snakes for nearly a half century. He has also indirectly saved thousands of lives. If you're bitten by a rattlesnake anywhere in America, it's almost certain the hospital will give you an antidote that started in Haast's lab. He's also a leading international provider of venom for research.

For four decades he and his snakes, sometimes as many as 10,000, performed for admiring tourists at the Miami Serpentarium. In 1984, he closed the attraction and moved lock, stock, and rattle to a research center in Utah.

But the snakes didn't fancy snow-skiing weather, so after about six years Haast bought 44 acres near Florida's

Palm Beach Post

"Snake Man" William Haast has been bitten more than 150 times.

Gulf Coast in Charlotte County.

There he continues to extract venom for his clients in a sprawling compound that will eventually include his home, a laboratory, and open snake pits.

Not everyone is happy Haast and his fanged friends are here.

"How would you like 1,000 poisonous snakes living next to you?" neighbor Brian Hall said.

Haast has done groundbreaking, and controversial, work in the use of venom to treat diseases. And he has spent his life trying to change stereotypes about snakes and slow their disappearance under the juggernaut of development.

HE LIVED TO TELL ABOUT IT

Trim, clothed in a white outfit, Haast looks much younger than his years — he was 87 in 1997 — as if each time he cheated death he won back some of his youth in the deal.

He has been bitten at least 150 times, half of the bites by cobras. Some are bites no one else has ever survived. His gnarled hands show the effects of the venom — a part of the snake's digestive juices that starts deteriorating human muscle almost immediately after contact.

In 1954, he was bitten by a krait — a snake with venom that is, drop for drop, 15 times more lethal than a cobra's venom. For a time after the bite, Haast was paralyzed and could not salivate or move his eyelids. He hallucinated, seeing visions of purple curtains, lambs' heads, opening doors, and moving furniture.

Haast's snakes range in size and deadliness from common Florida rattlers to king cobras, vipers, and two– to four-foot kraits.

Haast is the primary supplier to Wyeth Laboratories, which has virtually a monopoly on snake-bite antidotes. Wyeth injects small amounts of venom into horses, whose blood builds up antibodies. The blood is then safely removed and solids are separated. The solids are later reconstituted and injected into victims.

Wyeth buys 500 grams a year from Haast of each of four kinds of rattlesnake venom. From that the company creates 40,000 doses — 10 doses per snakebite victim.

There are other clients. Haast milks 1,500 copperheads a year for a Swiss pharmaceutical firm. For almost a pint of coral snake venom, he had to make 69,000 collections over three years. One gram of sea snake venom cost $10,000 and required 800 collections in Japan.

The job has its hazards, as newspaper clippings attest:

Haast Bitten by Snake Again.
Snake Handler "Critical."
Snake Bite, His 95th, Shrugged Off by Man.

He lives because in 1948 he started injecting himself with venom from up to 50 different snakes. He started with venom diluted one part in 10,000 and now takes booster shots every two weeks containing enough venom to kill five people.

Haast's blood is like gold to other snake-bite victims, and some two dozen have been saved by transfusions of his blood.

SAVING LIVES

Haast had already become interested in snakes before he got his first bite at the age of 16 while on a scout trip. Three years later, the New Jersey high school dropout linked up with a traveling snake show that landed him in South Florida. Surrounded by swamps, he decided to build his own snake farm. Nearly two decades of odd jobs passed before Haast was able to open his Miami Serpentarium in 1946.

Until he could make a living at it, he invited tourists in order to pay the bills. In the 1950s and 1960s, before Walt Disney World became the center of the tourism universe and when attractions lured tourists off the beach up and down Florida's coastline, the Serpentarium drew up to 50,000 people a year.

Tragedy struck in 1977 when a six-year-old West Palm Beach boy fell over a three-foot retaining wall into a pit and was killed by a 12-foot African crocodile named Cookie. Haast, fearing Cookie would become a ghoulish attraction, shot the animal.

In the late 1970s, Haast squared off with the U.S. Food and Drug Administration over a serum called PROven, which he developed from venom. He says it can help treat multiple sclerosis and other neurological disorders.

Haast and a doctor administered the serum to as many

as 6,000 patients at a South Florida clinic. Experts swore either that it was a godsend or worthless.

A facility in Mexico administers the drug and patients can bring it into the United States, but Haast is barred from producing or selling PROven in America.

Eventually the Serpentarium's attendance dropped to about 25,000 a year, and Haast accepted an offer from the University of Utah to continue his research and venom production.

The attraction's fixtures were auctioned off, and its landmark 32-foot concrete cobra was donated to a local high school that had a cobra as its mascot. The place was then bulldozed to make way for a shopping center.

In Utah, Haast found dry, cold, thin air did not agree with him or his snakes, most of them from tropical climates. So Haast and his assistant for 25 years, Nancy Harrell, loaded the snakes on trailers in April 1990 and returned to Florida.

The reception was not warm.

After reading a newspaper report, the area's property owners' group wrote Charlotte County Commissioner William Noel Jr., "to express in the most vigorous terms our concern and, indeed, horror."

"You've got the most venomous snakes in the world concentrated in one location," Noel said. "Florida's an ideal habitat. They could go forth and multiply."

Miami Serpentarium Laboratories: 34879 Washington Loop Road, Punta Gorda, FL 33982. Call (941) 639-8888.

PART II

HISTORY AIN'T PRETTY:

BLOOPERS, BUFFOONS, AND BOZOS IN FLORIDA'S PAST

There's a fellow in Central Florida who does tire commercials. "Tires ain't pretty," he says.

Many people get a view of history as a venue for glorious wars, landmark government actions, and dramatic figures making timeless speeches before hushed audiences. But the truth is, a lot of history ain't pretty either.

Florida, where the tacky is as much a part of the state's legacy as anything else, has had its share of bloopers, buffoons, and bozos along with the sweeping battles and dramatic political events.

THE STATE SEAL FROM HELL

On May 21, 1985, the state Legislature adopted a new version of the state seal. It seems previous ones had some embarrassing mistakes.

Legislators got rid of the portrayal of coffee, which was never a prime Florida crop. They replaced the cocoa palm with the sabal palm, which was, after all, the state tree. They clothed the Indian maiden in the dress of the Seminoles, rather than of the Indians from the Great Plains.

But the greatest gaffe was this: mountains in the background. Considering the highest point in Florida is a mere 345 feet above sea level, they represented a goof as big as a mountain.

Florida's State Seal showed mountains. Huh?

A SYMPATHETIC EAR

In the mid-1700s, the British coveted Spanish Florida and were just looking for an excuse to mix it up with the Spaniards. It came in the form of a human ear.

At least that was the story of smuggler Robert Jenkins, who said the disgusting thing he pulled from his pocket was his ear, hacked off by Spaniards when they boarded his boat off the Florida coast.

The British Parliament was aghast. Such an affront to a citizen of the realm would not go unpunished, they shouted. In 1740, England invaded Spanish-held Florida.

"The War of Jenkins' Ear" stemmed from a rather shaky argument. First of all, Jenkins' mutilation had come seven years earlier, and it was later shown he had lost his ear by other means and had merely displayed a piece of rabbit skin to the Parliament. But it was enough for the British.

The invasion failed, but England got Florida two decades later.

HI. SWIM HERE OFTEN?

The early Spanish explorers were brutal, bloodthirsty, and ambitious. Not all of them were good judges of beauty. Maybe it was the weeks at sea. But many now agree the legend of the beautiful mermaid, endowed with a glorious upper half but a fish from the waist down, stems from sailors' sightings of homely manatees.

Did sailors see manatees as mermaids?

WILL WORK FOR FOOD AND A TRIP TO FLORIDA

In the 1760s, a man named Denys Rolle recruited settlers for a town near Palatka. These were no Puritans. They included 200 of London's finest vagrants, bums, and debtors. Not being the most stable of people, when times got tough, they abandoned the settlement.

AND I THOUGHT IT WAS ME WHO SMELLED

After a while, America grew covetous of northeast Florida. You'd never know it from the way President James Monroe described Fernandina Beach — an area so filled with pirates, thieves and smugglers that it was "a festering fleshpot."

One day there rose from the horizon a ship bearing a white flag with a green cross. It was that of the mercenary Sir General Gregor MacGregor. Claiming five boats and a thousand men, MacGregor took Fernandina from the Spanish without a shot. He marched some of his troops through the town with tall poles bearing their flags. Everyone quickly figured out the poles were stalks of a smelly plant called dog fennel.

Florida Photographic Archives

Gregor MacGregor's army stunk

It turned out MacGregor really had only 150 men. His plan was to take North Florida from Spain and turn it over to the United States. When U.S. aid did not come, he slinked off.

SORRY, THE PRESIDENT CANNOT ACCEPT A COLLECT CALL

MacGregor was not the first to seize Northeast Florida. In 1812 the East Florida Patriots grabbed Florida from Spain and declared it "The Republic of East Florida." Its flag was a silhouette of a soldier and bayonet; the legend means "safety, the supreme law of the people."

The Patriots planned to later "surrender" to the United States, which had put them up to it. Spain protested and President James Madison said he'd never heard of the "Patriots." Alone, they lasted a few months.

SALUS POPULI LEX SUPREMA

Florida Department of State

Brown Brothers

The East Florida Patriots were left hanging by President Madison

A PROUD TRADITION

In 1819, Spain sold Florida to the fledgling United States for five million dollars. Actually, America agreed to take on five million dollars in claims by Americans living under the Spanish crown who had suffered various torts. But the United States never paid off the claims. This was the first great Florida land scam and would set the standard for others.

IF YOU CAN'T SAY SOMETHING NICE . . .

Not everyone welcomed the Sunshine State. During debate on whether to bring Florida into the United States, there were few detractors with pleas as stirring as U.S Congressman John Randolph of Virginia.

He called Florida "a land of swamps, of quagmires, of frogs and alligators and mosquitoes" and said no one would want to emigrate there, even from Hell.

IF YOU CAN'T SAY SOMETHING NICE, PART TWO

Poet Ralph Waldo Emerson got in his licks, too, once describing North Florida's St. Johns River as "grotesque."

MOON OVER FORT FOSTER

Once America gained Florida, it started doing what it had started to do across the continent: taking the Indians' land. While there's nothing funny about that tragedy, there were a few embarrassing moments for both sides.

The winner in the category of most clever nineteenth-century fraternity prank goes to a group of Seminoles who were laying siege to Fort Cooper, in Citrus County. The Indians decided to really tick off the soldiers inside and goad them into using up their ammunition. So they mooned the fort. The infuriated soldiers used up a lot of their bullets but not all of them. The man in charge was too smart for that. But the soldiers abandoned the fort after only 16 days to head to Fort Brooke, and the Indians moved in anyway.

WAY TO DESTROY GOVERNMENT PROPERTY

The best botched-suicide award has to go to the keeper of the Cape Florida lighthouse. On July 23, 1836, the light-house was attacked by Seminoles who set its base afire. Trapped on the top floor, the keeper decided there was only one way out: to light the dynamite stored there and blow up himself and the Indians, allowing him to be quick-fried instead of slow-roasted and making him a martyr. The thunderous explosion killed many of the

The Cape Florida lighthouse almost blew up

Seminoles and scared off the rest. It also put out the fire. When the smoke had cleared, the lighthouse was saved, and there was a dazed but alive lighthouse keeper.

ALAS, POOR COACOOCHEE. I KNEW HIM, HORATIO

In January 1841, soldiers at a fort near St. Augustine were surprised to find a group of Indians clad in the colorful outfits of a Shakespearean theatrical troupe. The Seminoles — led by Coacoochee, also known as Wildcat — attacked the group while it was touring frontier Florida. Four men were killed. The troupe moved on and finished its tour to packed houses.

FAMOUS LAST WORDS

On December 28, 1835, after trekking through Central Florida's Green Swamp for days, the estimated 100 troops under Maj. Francis Dade were exhausted and filthy. "Have a glad heart; our difficulties and dangers are over now . . ." Dade said. Soon, their troubles would indeed be over, as would their lives at the hands of the Seminoles.

The massacre helped spark the Second Seminole War and earned Dade the dubious distinction of having a county named after him posthumously. He probably would have preferred living to an old age in anonymity.

YEAH, BUT WOULD IT HAVE BEEN PINCKNEY VICE?

Dade's magnanimity in getting himself killed saved South Florida decades of embarrassment. Dade County, recently renamed Miami-Dade County, has become as well known as Chicago's Cook County and Atlanta's Fulton County. But could you imagine national television anchors reporting the actions of the "Pinckney" County Commission? Just as the Florida Legislature was preparing to name the county Pinckney — after a U.S. senator from Maryland who had championed slave-holding states during debates on the Missouri Compromise — word came of Dade's heroic demise.

THANKS BUT NO THANKS

The depression certainly didn't spare Florida's Seminoles. In 1936 the Indians, reeling with the rest of the country, had a historic meeting in the Everglades with Governor David Scholtz. To his offers of help they replied, "pohoan checkish." It means "leave us alone."

YOU DIRTY RAT!

Early in the twentieth century tourism and migration were contributing to the state's boom. Cities started springing up, and people came up with clever names for them, although not always in an orthodox manner.

Perhaps the most colorful town name in Florida is Boca Raton. Hispanics must shake their heads in amazement at a place named Mouth of the Mouse.

It was originally Boca de los Ratones — Mouth of the Mice. In this case the translation referred to an inlet — a mouth — with sharp rocks that, like rats' teeth, gnawed the ropes of ships rocking at anchor along the shore.

The Boca Raton Historical Society says there was, in fact,

such an inlet. But it was not in southern Palm Beach County. It was at Miami Beach. Mapmakers inadvertently placed the town where it is now.

MAPS? WE DON'T NEED NO STINKIN' MAPS!

Palm Beach is known for glitz, but it's also had its share of drunken binges. One led to the origin of the town's name. On January 9, 1878, the ship *Providencia* was bound from Trinidad to Cadiz, Spain, loaded with cargo. Not gold, silver, or jewels, but coconuts — 20,000 of them. The sailors had dipped into the grog a bit during the voyage, and before they knew it the ship had grounded on the coast of what is now Palm Beach. Local residents rushed to the beach. The tipsy crew thought the ship had landed in Mexico. Once they realized where they were, they decided the ship could not go on with its cargo. They sold the coconuts at the salvage price of two and a half cents each. The residents planted coconuts everywhere. Within a decade, the area was filled with palm trees, and the island had a new name: Palm Beach.

courtesy Preservation Foundation of Palm Beach
Eldred Clark Johnson,

The wreck of the *Providencia* gave Palm Beach its name

IF YOU'VE SEEN ONE INDIAN, YOU'VE SEEN THEM ALL

Many Florida towns were first developments and have been saddled with whatever name the builder wanted to place on them. The man who built Tequesta, near Jupiter in northern Palm Beach County, thought it would be neat to name it after a long-gone Florida Indian tribe. There was only one problem: the Tequesta had lived down around Miami. Even after a local historian explained the mix-up, the guy wouldn't budge.

NO, BUT WE HAVE IT IN FROZEN CONCENTRATE

In the 1880s, when Citrus County was formed north of Tampa, it was home to a flourishing citrus industry. But hard freezes over the next decade wiped out the groves and drove growers south. Now Citrus County has no citrus.

JUST THINK. IT COULD HAVE BEEN "WAY DOWN UPON THE CROSS-FLORIDA BARGE CANAL."

Stephen F. Foster's "Old Folks at Home," which is best known for its opening line, "Way down upon the Swanee river . . ." is the official state song. But Foster never saw North Florida's Suwannee River. His brother picked it from an atlas for its melodic name, which he shortened. He rejected his brother's first choices — South Carolina's Pee Dee and Mississippi's Yazoo.

EXCUSE ME. ARE THOSE YOUR BONES?

As the twentieth century boom progressed, more than one real estate huckster was willing to stoop low to get publicity. One day the esteemed Smithsonian Institution got a letter from a man in Pinellas County who explained excitedly that he'd uncovered bones from an ancient Indian settlement. Scientists raced to Florida, took one look, and quickly saw they had been victims of a hoax. Turns out the man had planted the bones and other items. As long as they were there, they decided, they might as well dig. They then found a major archaeological site, the Weedon

Island site, under the bones scattered by the con man.

THEY'RE NOT DEAD. THEY'RE JUST RESTING.

Naturalist John James Audubon is famed for his detailed illustrations of Florida's unusual wildlife. But how did he get all those birds and other animals to sit still? Many of his followers may be shocked to learn that Audubon, whose name has become synonymous with preservation, decided the easiest way to get them to stay put was to kill them and prop them up.

John James Audubon made sure his animals stood still. Real still.

SUNBURN? HOW ABOUT A WINDBURN?

In 1925, a national group of bankers was invited to hold its convention in St. Petersburg. The idea was to have them enjoy fun in the sun, then go back North and rave about Florida, thus encouraging investment. The bankers came on down. But instead of lying in the sun they played cards in their room and looked out the window. For three days the area was plagued by cold and rain. The bankers returned North and bad-mouthed Florida. It was one more nail in the coffin that was the real estate crash.

I LOVE FLORIDA SO MUCH I COULD KILL MYSELF

FAMOUS FLORIDA SUICIDES:

✗ John Milton, April 1, 1865: The Florida governor during the Civil War and descendant of the famed poet was a proud Southerner who had said in his last speech to the legislature, "Death would be preferable to reunion." As occupying federal troops headed for Tallahassee, Milton traveled to his Marianna plantation, retired to an upstairs bedroom, and put a bullet in his head. He was 57.

Governor John Milton: "Death would be preferable to reunion"

✗ Hamilton Disston, April 30, 1896: Part of the Disston family saw-manufacturing fortune, he was lured to Florida in 1881 and made the deal of a lifetime. He bought four million acres of Central Florida — a 6,200-square-mile chunk that ran from Kissimmee to Sanford, including the future site of Disney World — and about 11 percent of the state's total land area. His cost: one million dollars — 25 cents an acre. Disston began draining the land for farming and building, but an economic panic in 1893 wiped him out, and he killed himself in his native Philadelphia. He was 51.

Hamilton Disston drained Florida, then killed himself

✗ Frank Stranahan, May 22, 1929: The man called Fort Lauderdale's first white settler when he arrived in 1893 was ruined when South Florida's roaring '20s boom crashed. With creditors bearing down, he tied tiles around his waist and dove into the New River. He was 65.

✗ Jim Morrison, July 3, 1971: The Melbourne-native leader of The Doors came to epitomize the flawed genius and "up yours" stance of 1960s youth. On March 1, 1969, he allegedly exposed himself at a concert at the Dinner Key Auditorium in Miami's Coconut Grove neighborhood. The incident sparked a "Rally for Decency" in the Orange Bowl that drew 30,000 people. It featured entertainer Jackie Gleason, not the first person you think of at a rally for decency, and Anita Bryant, who would later become an antigay, profamily values crusader. Morrison, meanwhile, was convicted, but the case was on appeal when he drowned in a Paris bathtub. He was 27.

Broward County Historical Commission

Frank Stranahan, dogged by creditors, jumped into the New River

REST IN PEACE

Circus magnate John Ringling, of Ringling Brothers fame, built the palatial "Ca 'D' Zan" estate in Sarasota, now a historic site. According to legend, Ringling won possession of St. Armand's Key — now a chic resort and shopping spot — in a poker game. When Ringling died of pneumonia in 1936, his body and that of his wife — who had died seven years earlier — were placed in temporary crypts in New Jersey. Relatives squabbling over control of the Ringling estate could not decide where to put them permanently. So, in April 1987, they were secretly moved to unmarked crypts in an unnamed Southwest Florida cemetery. They were finally buried on the Ringling Museum grounds in June 1991.

Ringling was the most prominent of several Floridians who found fame even after death:

✗ Carl Fisher, the Indianapolis industrialist credited with putting Miami Beach on the map, wanted to be interred on Fisher Island, just off Miami Beach. He had a mausoleum built there. But he never got into it. When Fisher died in July 1939, his family took his ashes back home to the Fisher vault in Indiana. The Fisher Island crypt lay unused for six decades and was finally leveled.

Carl Fisher wasn't buried in his mausoleum

✗ No one is buried in William Brickell's Mausoleum, facing Biscayne Bay in downtown Miami. In fact the eight crypts built by the pioneer family are all vacant. Descendants moved the bodies when the city built up too much around the site.

✗ William "Fatty" Palmer was said to be the fattest man in Miami in the 1920s. He weighed 528 pounds. With a white beard and large hat, he sold trinkets outside the city's post office. He eventually had to live in a specially designed cottage on the county farm. He needed a system of ropes and pulleys so he could turn. At the time of his death, Palmer's weight had dropped to 300 pounds, but he still needed a specially designed casket. It was six feet long, 50 inches wide, and 22 inches deep and was said to be the largest ever used in the city.

✗ Carrie Miller, who was suffering from high blood pressure and was warned she could die at any moment, became intrigued by a magazine article about Pompeii, the ancient city covered by volcano ash. She noted that people were found frozen in place by the sudden eruption. Made wealthy when her family sold property that would house the University of Miami, Miller decided on an unusual burial. After her death on November 30, 1926, she was carried, bed and all, to a concrete slab in Miami's City Cemetery. There, concrete was poured over her body, forming a solid block that exists today. A planned bronze case with plate glass windows and a bronze bust of Mrs. Miller on it never happened.

REST IN THE MIDDLE OF THE STREET
Charles Dummett, killed in an 1860 hunting accident, was buried in a quiet New Smyrna Beach neighborhood. In the 1960s, the legal complexities of moving the 16-year-old's grave led developers to leave it where it was and split a new city street around it. But historians said vandals have done so much damage to the 30-square-foot concrete monument that they doubt Dummett is still there.

OCCUPATIONAL HAZARDS
George End and a partner founded a rattlesnake-meat canning operation and tourist stand in the 1930s on the Gandy Bridge from Tampa to St. Petersburg. One day, one of his inventory brought an early end to Mr. End.

TAKING THE LAW INTO YOUR OWN HANDS
In 1920, Palm Beach County State Attorney Edgar C. Thompson convinced a judge in an Okeechobee bootlegger's case that he, as the bootlegger's attorney, should hold the contraband for safekeeping. He and a deputy loaded it

in his Model T and set out for West Palm Beach. When the grand jury next met, the evidence had disappeared. A few days later, Gov. Sidney J. Catts suspended Thompson for "public drunkenness and neglect of official duties." Remarkably, Thompson was reelected and the governor, opting for discretion, restored him to office.

DIVORCE COURT, PART ONE
On September 7, 1922, a woman successfully annulled her Miami marriage by explaining that although Prohibition was in effect, she was drunk the night of August 22 and did not realize she was in the middle of a wedding ceremony. She said she awakened the next morning in a West Palm Beach hotel and remembered she was engaged to someone else.

DIVORCE COURT, PART TWO
In their 1941 divorce, Eleanor McCaul asked a court to deny her husband, Thomas, visitation rights to their dog. She said her husband had never supported the pet and had no right to see it.

WHAT DO YOU WEAR TO A ROBBERY?
The Ashley gang was a group of ruthless bandits that terrorized South Florida in the early part of this century. But they apparently were not without a sense of humor. In May 1922, members of the gang robbed a bank in Stuart. Their leader was dressed in women's clothing.

SHOOT? DID SOMEONE SAY SHOOT?
One of the most dramatic moments in law enforcement history was the five-and-a-half-hour shootout that ended in the deaths of gangsters Ma and Fred Barker on January 16, 1935, at a quiet lakefront vacation cabin in Ocklawaha, near Ocala. They were tracked down after authorities found a penciled circle on a map at an earlier hideout. Decades later, Ocala Police Chief McGehee interviewed two of the agents who were there. McGehee is now

convinced the Barkers were killed in the first 45-minute barrage and that jumpy agents later shot any time something moved.

DID YOU PILOTS ONCE WORK FOR THE FBI IN OCKLAWAHA?

During World War II, the little town of Frostproof — just north of the Avon Park Bombing Range — had only one intersection, which had a street light at each corner. From the air, it resembled a giant "X." Several times during night training errant pilots bombed Frostproof.

YEAH, BUT IT GOT GREAT MILEAGE

On June 25, 1951, Julia St. Clair and her son arrived in California, 13 months after leaving Jacksonville. They made the 2,500-mile journey on foot. The woman pushed 135 pounds of food, clothing, and a cat in a wheelbarrow.

TALK ABOUT FAINT PRAISE!

Lee Weissenborn is honored with a plaque in no less hallowed a place than the new Florida capitol building. The state senator from Miami wanted to move the capital to Orlando, a place many people believe makes more sense,

Lee Weissenborn kept the Capital in Tallahassee. Sort of.

as Florida has become more bottom-heavy. The idea of losing state government and its economic impact so frightened the powers that be that they were spurred to build the new capitol center in Tallahassee. And they hung a plaque to Weissenborn, without whose efforts the new building never would have happened.

AND YOU THOUGHT "LIBERAL" WAS A DIRTY WORD

There have been many great battles in Florida history but perhaps none to match those in the arena of politics.

One of the most infamous quotes — or misquotes — in political history is the nefarious "nepotism" tirade attributed to George Smathers in the 1950 U.S. Senate Democratic primary, a campaign perhaps unmatched for sleaze.

Smathers reportedly said: "Are you aware that Claude Pepper is known all over Washington as a shameless extrovert? Not only that, but this man is reliably reported to practice nepotism with his sister-in-law, and he has a sister who was once a thespian in wicked New York. Worst of all, it is an established fact that Mr. Pepper, before his marriage, habitually practiced celibacy."

Naive voters were horrified by the double-talk and picked Smathers by 67,000 votes. He easily defeated his Republican opponent in the general election. Smathers

The Smathers-Pepper race was one of the ugliest in history

denied the quotes alleged to him and many now believe
he never uttered them. But the perceived travesty of political justice stayed with both men.

NOW HERE'S A SHAMELESS EXTROVERT
On May 28, 1931, Legislator John E. Matthews got up to
speak on the floor of the Florida House of Representatives.
He didn't sit down for seven hours and 45 minutes. In
fact, he set a one-day filibuster record en route to a 19-
hour talkathon that ended in a Matthews win and a fist-
fight on the floor of the House.

BRILLIANT POLICE WORK, CONGRESSMAN
The ABSCAM scandal, in which politicians were caught
taking bribes from undercover agents posing as Arab
sheiks, brought down Tampa Bay Congressman Richard
Kelly, who was seen on videotape stuffing $25,000 in $20
and $100 bills into his pockets in January 1980 and ask-
ing, "Does it show?" Later, in a television interview, he
explained that "ten thousand dollars in new hundred-dol-
lar bills is little more than a half-inch thick" and said he
put the cash in the glove compartment of his car, then in
a file cabinet, and spent $174 for small purchases like
lunches. He finally gave the rest back to the FBI. He said
he thought the sheiks were crooks, and he took the money
as part of his own investigation. Kelly went to prison.

NOW BOYS, DON'T FIGHT
On January 23, 1894, soldiers marched into Jacksonville —
not to put down a rebellion, as in the Civil War, but to stop
a confrontation between heavyweights "Gentleman Jim"
Corbett and Charles Mitchell. The mayor and governor,
morally opposed to the blood sport, had ordered the match
called off, but promoters wouldn't budge. British challenger
Mitchell was arrested on his arrival but posted bond. A local
lawyer stopped an injunction, and the militia backed off.
The fight went on in a blinding rain. Corbett won in a
knockout. Criminal charges against both men failed to stick.

HIS NEXT FIGHT IS JIM CORBETT
Ernest Hemingway might have been a Nobel Prize–winning author, but Miss Manners he wasn't. For years he wrote, drank, fished, and lived the tropical lifestyle at his home at 907 Whitehall Street in Key West. It was there that Hemingway, surrounded by his famous six-toed cats, wrote *Death in the Afternoon, Green Hills of Africa* and *To Have and Have Not,* and began *For Whom the Bell Tolls.* One night at a party for the town's large colony of litterati, Hemingway's sister struck up a conversation with poet Wallace Stevens. He told her he didn't think much of her brother's work, upsetting her almost to tears. Papa stormed into the party, called Stevens outside, and broke his jaw with a single right hook. Both men would later win Pulitzer Prizes.

HEMINGWAY FOR PRESIDENT
In 1982, after a drug roadblock stopped traffic on U.S. 1 — isolating the Keys — Key West declared its "independence," threw a giant party, and began a lucrative trade in "Conch Republic" souvenirs that continues to this day.

A CREDIT TO THE COMMUNITY
In April 1962, engineer Minas Edward Nicolaides was declared the millionth resident of Miami's burgeoning Dade County. It turned out later he'd grown up in Dade and moved away in 1950. Four months after his 1962 honor, embarrassed chamber of commerce officials learned he'd left for a better job in Arizona — and, to add insult to injury, was bad-mouthing his former home. "The humidity chokes you," he told *Life* magazine. "I've still got green mold on my shoes."

PATIENCE, PATIENCE
On April 24, 1974, a new professional sports entity came into being. It was the Tampa Bay Buccaneers. In the NFL football team's first season, in 1976, it failed to win any of its 14 games.

MAYBE THE WORMS CAN START FOR THE BUCS
Every July, the small Florida community of Caryville holds its worm-fiddling festival. Participants drive a stake in the ground, then vibrate it to force the worms to the surface.

WHAT DO YOU GET FOR A POSTCARD WITH AN ALLIGATOR BITING A GIRL ON THE BOTTOM?
On January 25, 1925, the glorious Hialeah racetrack opened for business on a 200-acre site. The fun didn't last long. By May the state legislature had outlawed gambling, declaring it a felony and calling for a five-year prison term for offenders and what was then a hefty fine of $5,000. The Hialeah folks kept operating. They sold postcards of horses. If the horse on your card won, the track bought the card back at a premium price that just happened to match the winning odds.

Hialeah Racetrack had lucrative postcards

HUNDREDS OF PEOPLE SAW LINCOLN GET SHOT, AND THEY'RE ALL DEAD. HMMM.
On the thirtieth anniversary of the John F. Kennedy assassination, conspiracy buffs continued to have a field day with the Florida connections to the slaying:

✗ In early November 1963, a Miami police intelligence officer recorded a right-wing organizer saying Kennedy would be shot with a high-powered rifle from a tall building. The detective warned the FBI.

✗ Lee Harvey Oswald's reported mentor in Dallas, Russian exile George de Mohrenschildt, retired to Manalapan, near Palm Beach. In 1977, a House committee investigator came to his home to pursue allegations he was Oswald's CIA contact. The investigator left his card. De Mohrenschildt got home, put the card in his pocket, and shot himself.

✗ New Orleans district attorney Jim Garrison subpoenaed Cuban exile and Miami resident Eladio Del Vallea. Before Vallea could testify, he was murdered.

✗ Johnny Rosselli, a mobster with CIA connections, said Cuban leader Fidel Castro was behind the assassination. In August 1976, before the House committee could call him as a witness, Rosselli's body was found floating in a barrel in Biscayne Bay.

SURPRISE, SURPRISE
When workers on Henry Flagler's railroad to Key West got to a body of water just north of Key Largo, they thought it would be a cinch to build a causeway in the six-foot depth. They learned the bottom was soft peat. It took 15 months to build a one-mile embankment. The lake was dubbed "Lake Surprise."

GOOD THING SHE DIDN'T TRY TO CROSS LAKE SURPRISE
In 1973, a 25-year-old mother of four, homesick for Arkansas, hijacked a two-million-dollar, 28-car train during a crew change in the Sanford switching yards. At Pierson, in northwest Volusia County, a brakeman sent the stolen train onto a siding, where it struck a gondola and derailed. The woman told arresting police it was her first train ride. It had been 102 years since someone stole a train in Florida; police eventually opted to charge the

woman with grand theft. She pleaded insanity and went to a mental hospital.

GOOD THING SHE DIDN'T STEAL A TRAIN

In 1973, Madeline Dow, a 74-year-old from Toronto, was driving with three friends across the Treasure Island Causeway near St. Petersburg. She apparently didn't notice the flashing lights and warning bells. Next thing she knew, her 1962 Thunderbird was stuck on the lip of the rising drawbridge. It caught the underside of the car, keeping the four from going into the drink but trapping them 35 feet up. It took two hours for firefighters to rescue the women, who sued the city of Treasure Island.

PEACE, LOVE, ANTS, AND ALLIGATORS

Thousands of people will swear they were at Woodstock, the three-day celebration of peace, love, and music in upstate New York in 1969 that was both a symbol and one of the last hurrahs for the love generation of the 1960s.

Three and a half months later Florida had its own version of Woodstock. Like its bigger predecessor, this one got rained on.

The First Annual Palm Beach International Music and Arts Festival, held November 28–30, 1969, drew 40,000 people to a racetrack northwest of West Palm Beach. The list of acts was impressive — The Rolling Stones, Grand Funk Railroad, Janis Joplin, Iron Butterfly, Vanilla Fudge, Jefferson Airplane, Sly and the Family Stone.

But a freezing rain turned the place into a quagmire. Everything ran late. The last act, The Rolling Stones, appeared near dawn. And the sheriff admitted 20 years later that he had brought in red ants and alligators to encourage an early end.

RELAX, LEONARD. IT COULD HAVE BEEN THE SAME DEAL FRANCIS DADE GOT.

Jacksonville high school athletics coach Leonard Skinner made a habit of harassing a group of students for their long hair and manners. When the group formed into a rock-and-roll band, they named themselves for their high

Lynyrd Skynyrd honored their high school coach

school coach, without whom they'd never have become famous as Lynyrd Skynyrd.

TODAY, I AM THE 50-YARD LINE

Miami has long been known for garish glitz, but the Bar Mitzvah held in 1978 must be the all-time champion. Harvey Cohen's reception was held in the Orange Bowl with an orchestra, a 64-piece high school marching band, waitresses dressed as cheerleaders, bartenders as referees, and his name on the scoreboard. "I'll never forget it," Cohen, said in a 1992 *Miami Herald* article when he was 27. "I wish I could have that party now." But Miami Beach Rabbi Irving Lehrman remarked that the event was more "Bar" than "Mitzvah."

It was one of a string of outrageous Bar and Bat Mitzvahs:

✗ Gladys Matz, owner of several clothing shops, used a "Fantasy Island" theme for her daughter Jeanette, renting the *Miss Florida* ship. She rented parrots from Parrot Jungle and ordered a volcano-shaped cake that erupted. Midgets and Hawaiian girls gave boarding guests leis. Each of the 80 children got a live parakeet in a wooden cage with one day's food.

For her son Stanley, she did a "Barn Mitzvah," transforming the family's five-acre South Dade ranch into an Old West town, with a jail and tables covered in denim. Invitations were in burlap bags.

"When I do it, I do it," Matz said.

✗ The Boca Raton Bat Mitzvah reception for Taryn Glist of Hollywood opened with Whitney Houston singing "One Moment in Time" on a big screen. Her image froze, and Taryn, who aspired to be on Broadway, picked up where Houston left off, microphone in hand, as a video flashed highlights of the youngster's performing career. New York rabbi Jeffrey Salkin, author of *Putting God on the Guest List*, calls that "one of the low moments in Jewish-American history."

IS THIS THE STOP FOR THE TRI-RAIL?

The last blooper is actually a Florida folktale, one of many gathered by Florida State University professor J. Russell Reaver over four decades. But it might have happened. The train from Tallahassee was notorious for always pulling into Jacksonville late. One day it came in right on time, amazing the regulars. They swarmed the engineer, only to hear him sadly inform them that this was yesterday's train.

PART III

THE DAILY WEIRD:

BIZARRE FLORIDA BEHAVIOR FROM TODAY'S NEWSPAPERS

CELEBRITY CORNER

Broward County sheriff's deputy Jeffrey Willets and his wife, Kathy, were arrested in 1991 for running a prostitution and blackmail business in their apartment. Kathy was accused of bringing as many as eight men a day to her bedroom while her husband hid in the closet, taking notes or videotaping the encounters.

Miami lawyer Ellis Rubin, who made a name representing high-profile and offbeat clients, argued that Kathy became a nymphomaniac after taking the antidepressant drug Prozac and needed to have sex with men as therapy because her husband suffered from spells of impotence.

Jeffrey later pleaded guilty to a felony charge and quit the force. Kathy admitted misdemeanor counts in a plea agreement. The couple showed up on several television tabloid shows.

Three years later, Willets was arrested after her final, sellout performance at a West Palm Beach nude dancing lounge. But a judge dismissed a lewdness charge. Willets had argued her dance, which featured a razor and a red lightbulb, was a protected form of expression. Under the lewdness law, prosecutors had to prove her conduct offended people viewing it. "How are we going to find patrons to testify?" prosecutor Krista Rothman said. "They're paying $10 to get in. To them, the lewder the better."

Palm Beach Post, September 21, 1994

Television star Paul "Pee-wee Herman" Reubens was arrested at the South Trail Cinema, an adult movie house in Sarasota, while watching *Nancy Nurse, Tiger Shark,* and *Turn Up the Heat.* Two officers reported seeing the bearded Reubens sitting alone in a compromising position. CBS promptly canceled five "Pee-wee's Playhouse" reruns, Disney-MGM Studios pulled a video starring the bow-tied Pee-wee from a theme park tour, and an avalanche of Pee-wee jokes followed. Reubens later pleaded no contest and began a slow rehabilitation that eventually landed him a recurring role on the sitcom "Murphy Brown." In 1996, MGM/UA Entertainment gave Reubens a new comedy show after market research showed no lasting fallout from his ill-fated Sarasota adventure.

Palm Beach Post, July 13, 1993; November 25, 1996

Pee-wee Herman was caught without his bow tie

The U.S. Attorney for South Florida, Kendall Coffey, quit his post after he allegedly bit the arm of a topless dancer. Coffey, upset that his prosecutors had failed to convict two

Palm Beach Post

Did Kendall Coffey bite a stripper?

alleged top drug traffickers, reportedly went to the Lipstik Adult Entertainment Club, bought a magnum of champagne for about $900, and paid for a private dance, where he struggled with the woman and bit her.

Palm Beach Post, May 17, October 2, 1996

The 1997 murder of fashion designer Gianni Versace in Miami Beach brought out South Florida's usual nuttiness.

The same day Versace was gunned down, hawkers were seen rubbing Versace magazine ads on the sidewalk in front of his South Beach mansion, hoping to capture bloodstains.

Versace's alleged slayer, spree killer Andrew Cunanan, became the most wanted man in America and was sighted from one end of the country to the other. Eight days later, the caretaker of a houseboat moored two and a half miles from the murder scene called 911 to report a stranger. Police brought busy Collins Avenue to a stop for hours as they surrounded the houseboat. They finally rushed the boat and found Cunanan dead of an apparent self-inflicted gunshot wound.

The Miami Beach Police spokesman got demoted for initially saying no one was inside. Then 17 members of the Miami Beach SWAT team said they would quit because they were offended when the Metro-Dade team took over the storming of the houseboat.

The caretaker demanded a $45,000 reward, but authorities balked, saying he didn't know it was Cunanan he was reporting. The man got a lawyer and threatened to sue; residents flooded phone lines to support him. Authorities relented and gave him the reward. The boat later sank.

Meanwhile, Paul Philip, special-agent-in-charge for the Miami office of the FBI, had been paged at a black-tie benefit and raced to the scene just after the houseboat was stormed. As he stood among sweaty police officers and reporters, someone asked about his tuxedo. "My God, gentlemen," he said. "It is after six."

Palm Beach Post, July 25, 26, 31, 1997
Fort Lauderdale Sun-Sentinel, July 30, 1997

When police in Ocean Ridge, south of Palm Beach, found Spencer A. Wagner alone on the beach at four A.M., he told them he was "sorting out his personal problems." He then said he was with a woman. Officers then found Marla Maples Trump, then wife of Donald Trump, who explained that she couldn't find a public restroom and had told Wagner, her bodyguard, to pull over so she could use the beach. Trump and Maples later split up and Trump would sue the guard, saying he violated a sweeping confidentiality agreement by telling the *Globe* tabloid that he had had a tryst with Marla.

Palm Beach Post, December 30, 1996; May 30, November 1, 1997

On December 6, 1980, evangelist Jim Bakker had his now infamous rendezvous with church secretary Jessica Hahn in room 538 at the Sheraton Sand Key Resort in Clearwater Beach. Six and a half years later, his PTL ministry was rocked by revelations of the affair and that he paid Hahn hush money. Bakker left PTL, and he was later convicted of defrauding followers of $3.7 million and sentenced to 45 years in prison. Meanwhile, the enterprising hotel manager, after getting many visitors' requests to stay in the room, suggested putting the number on every room on the floor.

Wife Tammy Faye Bakker said that she was having trouble getting a place in Orlando to hold services for the Jim and Tammy Ministries. "Satan is trying to stop us from holding services in Florida," she said.

Palm Beach Post, December 31, 1987; *Orlando Sentinel*, December 31, 1989

The wife of deposed Panamanian strongman Manuel Noriega — on trial for allegedly amassing $23 million from dealings with cocaine traffickers — was arrested on shoplifting charges after she and a friend plucked 27 buttons, worth $305, from designer clothes in a Burdines store at Dadeland Mall in suburban Miami. Felicidad Noriega later agreed to a plea bargain in which she paid the store $1,320.94 for damages to the clothing.

Palm Beach Post, March 25, June 16, 1992

Dan Quayle, speaking in St. Petersburg, concluded a morning campaign speech with the line "And so, good night."

Orlando Sentinel, January 1, 1989

A 911 call to Brevard County dispatchers said Libyan leader Moammar Gadhafi was dining at a Merritt Island Denny's. Skeptical police showed up anyhow and found Michael Belman, a jeweler of Lebanese ancestry, eating with his three-year-old son. Belman said he had been taken for Gadhafi before.

Orlando Sentinel, March 1, 1989

For 439 days, from November 29, 1982, to January 21, 1984, H. David Weder lived inside a tin cylinder attached to a 30-foot pole atop the Jersey Jim Towers electronics store in Clearwater. The feat broke the *Guinness Book of World Records* record for pole-sitting. "He was verbally abusive to some people, and he wasn't clean," store owner Jim Towers Jr., said. "It was kind of like having a hobo move into your front lawn." Weder came down after Clearwater police threatened to blow him off his perch with a high pressure water hose.

Tampa Tribune, January 1, 1989

A woman found a Ken doll on a Toys 'R' Us shelf in north Tampa that was dressed in a purple tank top and lace skirt. Thinking she'd found a collector's item, she and the doll appeared on *The Joan Rivers Show* and in *Fortune* and *Newsweek* magazines. The woman was offered as much as $4,000 for her Ken. Within days, a store clerk admitted he had cross-dressed Ken late one night while goofing off. He was fired. His name: Ron Zero.

Associated Press/*Palm Beach Post*, August 23, 1990

THE PERFORMING ARTS

On Perdido Key, southwest of Pensacola, thousands have gathered every April since 1986 on the beach behind the Flora-Bama Bar for the four-day Mullet Toss. Contestants stand in a 10-foot circle right on the Florida-Alabama line and throw a one- to one-and-a-half-pound mullet — dead, of course — into Alabama. Participants are forbidden to wear gloves or rub sand on the fish to improve traction. Throws are judged for distance. Anything outside the 200-foot long, 25-foot-wide alley is a foul fish. Winners get prizes that include a mullet dinner for two. Former University of Alabama and NFL quarterback Ken Stabler, who grew up nearby, threw the first mullet ever — 81 feet — in 1986 and still tosses the ceremonial first mullet at each year's event. But he usually forgets to hold the torpedo-shaped fish by its tail and ends up grasping it by its abdomen like a football, forcing its insides out.

Palm Beach Post, October 18, 1993

Just a few miles and a few days away from downtown Miami's Orange Bowl Parade, the King Mango Strut in Coconut Grove pokes fun at the nationally famed event. The Strut began in 1981 and has featured such entries as the Marching Freds — 118 men and boys named Fred — and the Marching Barbies — takeoffs on America's most famous doll. The parade also featured "Pink Flamingos from Planet X" and King Mango's Ugliest Building in the Grove Contest.

United Press International/Orlando Sentinel, December 27, 1987

Orlando established the Queen Kumquat Sashay with the same idea as the King Mango Strut. The grand marshal the first year, 1986, was Longfellow, a champion cockroach. The second year it was a woman fired for mooning fellow employees at a Kissimmee boat company. Among entrants over the years: the World Famous Motley Crew Cavorting and Milling Society, the Sacred and Somewhat Vague Order of the Armadillo, the Society for Safe Sex, the Coalition for the Restoration of Common Courtesy (CROCC), and the World's Tallest Beehive Hairdo (it was almost seven feet tall).

Orlando Sentinel, November 8, 1987

A Lakeland television talk show host scolding officials for coming down on a student who had bared his bottom showed his support for the youth by mooning viewers.

Palm Beach Post, December 31, 1987

A Plant City man seeking a competency hearing on drug and theft charges peeled off his orange jail clothes and mooned a Bartow courtroom. "And I could have been a mullet fisherman," Circuit Judge E. Randolph Bentley groaned.

Orlando Sentinel, September 13, 1987

In Key West, a slightly intoxicated off-duty sailor mooned two women on their way to a party by climbing onto the hood of their car, pulling down his pants, and sitting on the front windshield. The windshield cracked, lacerating the sailor's posterior.

Orlando Sentinel, January 1, 1989

Florida passed a law in 1989 banning barroom dwarf-tossing contests, in which short people let others pick them up and see how far they can throw them for prize money.

"Dwarf-tossing may financially help the person who does it. However, it tears down the structure and the esteem that little people are trying to gain," Little People of America spokesman Ernie Ott said.

Groups also opposed dwarf-bowling, in which a helmeted dwarf strapped to a skateboard is used as a human bowling ball.

Orlando Sentinel, July 2, 1989

FLORIDA FAMILY VALUES

The Lobster Man trial turned a Tampa courtroom into a freak show.

Prosecutors said Grady Stiles Jr., the Lobster Man — nicknamed for a genetic deformity that left him with two-fingered, pincerlike hands and stunted, footless legs — was the victim of a murder conspiracy by his wife, Mary; his daughter Cathy Berry, born with the same deformities as her father; and his wife's stepson Harry Glenn Newman – "The Human Blockhead."

Mary Stiles claimed the plot was an act of self-defense. She said her husband was a drunken brute who battered and sexually abused her and threatened to kill her and her family.

Prosecutors said the cabal paid 19-year-old neighbor Christopher Wyant $1,500 to shoot Stiles twice in the back of the head in November 1992 as he sat watching television in his trailer in Gibsonton, a small town on the east side of Tampa Bay that's home to carnival workers.

Newman was sentenced to a life term, Mary Stiles 12 years, and Wyant 27 years.

"I'd do anything for my mother — anything," said the Blockhead, a 20-year-old who hammered nails into his nostrils for a living. "There ain't no price for my mother's love."

Palm Beach Post, July 28, August 9, August 30, October 15, 1994

Mary Grieco of Boynton Beach was convicted of murder in the famed "Couch Potato Murder." The woman was charged with crawling into bed and shooting her husband, Joe. Police say the couple's teenaged daughter and her boyfriend plotted the slaying with Mary Grieco for 10 weeks. The three said Joe Grieco was lazy and demanding and watched too much television; later they said Grieco also beat and sexually assaulted his wife and daughter.

Palm Beach Post, October 16, 1991

In 1988, Kimberly Mays became a national figure when it was revealed doctors at a Wauchula Hospital had switched her at birth with an ill child. After Regina and Ernest Twigg's child, Arlena, whom they raised as their own for nine years, died of a congenital heart illness, the couple sued Hardee Memorial Hospital. They claimed

Kimberly Mays: switched at birth

hospital records showed their daughter was born healthy on December 2, 1978. Tests showed Arlena had a blood type that couldn't match those of the Twiggs.

Palm Beach Post, September 8, 1988

Aileen Wuornos, a 35-year-old woman charged in the serial killings of five hitchhikers, was legally adopted by an Ocala couple. "We want her to know what it feels like to have a family that really cares about her," explained Arlene Pralle.

Palm Beach Post, December 31, 1991

Aileen Wuornos: Adopt-a-Murderer

A Palm Beach man sought an annulment of his 10-year-marriage, saying his wife never told him she was once a man. He said he'd have never married her had he known she had a sex change in 1970. The annulment would have kept him from paying alimony. The couple was eventually divorced.

Palm Beach Post, October 28, 1994

When a 41-year-old Bradenton man married an 18-year-old woman, both claimed they were surprised when prosecutors announced that the girl was the man's daughter. "We don't know if it's true," said Jimmy Hendry, who was charged with incest three months after marrying Trina Irene Heiser, "but if it is, I have to stop loving her as a husband and start loving her as a father. I can do that. There's different kinds of love." Authorities claim Hendry fathered Trina in Flint, Michigan, 19 years ago, while living with a woman whom they believe to be Trina's mother. "There's a right way and a wrong way for a father and child to be reunited," Hendry said. "This may be the worst way in the world." The woman finally left Hendry four years later after saying he had acknowledged being her father.

St. Petersburg Times, December 7, 1989; *Orlando Sentinel*, March 26, 1994

A three-year-old Land O' Lakes boy snuck into his sleeping parents' bedroom, climbed onto the dresser, stole their keys, and took the family car for a joyride. "I go zoom," he said. A month later, the boy ignited his bedroom curtains with a cigarette lighter and burned down the house. "The wood burned," Mikey explained. "Now I have no more house."

Palm Beach Post, December 29, 1993

A nine-year-old Mount Dora boy who was home alone with his four-year-old cousin fired more than a dozen shots out his window with a .22-caliber rifle before police took it away from him.

Orlando Sentinel, March 5, 1994

A Brooksville mother who needed money to enter her four-year-old daughter in a beauty pageant slit her boss' throat and robbed the safe of Bubbalou's Bodacious Bar-B-Que, police said. The boss survived the attack. Ann Marie Bloxsom returned an hour later, telling officers she wanted to surrender rather than be arrested in front of her child. "She's the kind of person who doesn't even spank our kid," husband Terry Bloxsom said.

Associated Press/*Palm Beach Post*, June 8, 1994

A mentally ill, 230-pound weightlifter in Hollywood was accused of crushing to death his 150-pound father with a bear hug. Neighbors said the father and son were very close, walking the neighborhood and eating meals together, but the son, who was manic-depressive, became moody when he was not on his medication.

Associated Press/*Orlando Sentinel*, November 9, 1988

As a Spanish-language television news crew tried to interview a woman at the Broward County grave of her teenage daughter, her ex-husband ran up and fatally shot her nine times in the head. The man was later arrested on a Greyhound bus in Texas. He apparently blamed his former wife for the suicide of their 15-year-old daughter.

Palm Beach Post, January 21, 1993

A mother threw her two-year-old son from the roof of a three-story federal courthouse in Miami, but the child landed on grass and survived.

Associated Press/*Orlando Sentinel*, September 26, 1987

A St. Petersburg woman said voices in her head directed her to bite off part of her four-year-old daughter's ear and finish the job with a butcher knife. Doctors were unable to reattach it because 16 hours passed before the ear was found. The woman was placed in a mental hospital.

Orlando Sentinel, November 14, 1987

A man was charged with keeping a couple and their daughter captive for 15 years. Roland and Sandra Cardin and their daughter, Michele, told police that Robert Mauro, who they met at a Connecticut flea market, beat them and kept them imprisoned by fear, convincing them that his friends in the Mob were constantly watching them. Before coming to Stuart in late 1989, they lived in Palm Beach and Broward Counties and Mount Dora. Mauro's public defender accused the Cardins of making up the hostage story so they could bilk him out of a painting. Mauro was never prosecuted in the hostage allegation — prosecutors wouldn't say why — but pleaded no contest to weapons and marijuana charges. Three years later, he was sentenced in New York to five and a half years in prison for beating and kicking his wife because he didn't like the dinner she'd served.

Palm Beach Post, April 10, 1991; March 2, 1994

The Lanting family of Palm Beach threw a $6,000 military-themed birthday party for 150 guests for their son Chase, catered by the ritzy Breakers Hotel. They recruited a half-dozen National Guardsmen in three Humvee vehicles who gave the guests personalized dog tags and buzz cuts, then stormed the home to "kidnap" Chase and gave him a real Purple Heart after his rescue. U.S. Representative Mark Foley, a Republican from West Palm Beach, called it a "foolish waste of time and tax dollars." Real Purple Heart recipients said it defiled the honor of their sacrifice. And local National Guard leaders threatened to demote the soldiers. The Chases said they meant no harm.

Palm Beach Post, December 19, 1935

A Pensacola radio station offered a "Gulf Coast Breeders Cup" and $1,000 to the first of three couples to conceive a child in a contest aimed at higher ratings. "We thought, 'Why do another car giveaway?'" WTKX program director Mike Ondayko said. The station said it would give the finalists "love enhancers:" a water bed, a night in a hotel, a seafood buffet, a gift certificate from a lingerie shop, champagne, candles, and green M&Ms.

St. Petersburg Times, November 2, 1990

Will Bellin, headmaster of a Savannah, Georgia, Lutheran school, brought 15 students to Central Florida for a field trip. Bellin's wife, Sharon, cut short a tour of Epcot Center and went to a walk-in clinic, complaining of lower back pain she blamed on the five-hour drive. "Wrong," the doctors said, "you're in labor." Hours later she delivered the couple's first child. "We had sort of given up on having a family," said Will Belin. The couple had been married for eight years. Sharon had recently experienced a small weight gain but was a large woman; the couple said they had no idea she was pregnant.

Orlando Sentinel, May 26, 1989

Doug and Barbara Montgomery of West Palm Beach received a letter from Lake Worth High School saying their son, Bill, had been suspended for three days after disrupting the class and calling his teacher an obscene name. Bill, however, was 30 years old and had never even attended the school. The mix-up was blamed on a computer glitch.

Palm Beach Post, December 30, 1996.

A Boca Raton woman called police one night to say her husband had been missing since he went to the post office that afternoon. Authorities called back with good news and bad news; her husband was safe — in jail. U.S. marshals had arrested him on Illinois sexual assault charges.

Boca Raton Police, February 5, 1997

SEX

Two married FBI agents accosted by a robber outside a swingers, club shot the man to death. They were later fired for being members of the club. Frank and Suzanne Monserrate were confronted as they left the private sex club in southern Miami-Dade County about two A.M. by a gunman who ripped gold chains from their necks and shot Suzanne in the back. The two said the inquiry into their private lives that ensued, and their subsequent dismissal, violated their constitutional rights to privacy.

Fort Lauderdale Sun-Sentinel; January 5, 7, 19, 1987; November 26, 1987

At a condominium complex in North Tampa, a neighbor videotaped a couple having sex behind their open mini-blinds, supposedly in view of neighborhood children. The couple was arrested on felony lewdness charges. Later, they were charged with three counts of disorderly conduct — for having sex in the condo hot tub, for swimming seminaked in the pool, and for having sex in a restaurant bathroom. They also became instant stars, appearing on *Donahue, The Maury Povich Show, Larry King Live,* and in a segment on *A Current Affair* titled "Leer Window."

Orlando Sentinel, May 28, 1992

A Boca Raton woman complained to police that her next-door neighbor's bed was against her dining room wall and that she "hears excessive banging when intimate relations are occurring." Police told the woman they couldn't do anything unless an officer was in the home and heard the banging. They advised her that the couple's lease was up in four months, and she'd have to put up with the noise until they moved out.

Boca Raton Police, September 11, 1997

Before getting in the shower, Darleen Scott of Palm Springs told her daughters to get her if her favorite video came on TV. So when Gladys Knight's "Love Overboard" came on, Scott raced from the shower to the living room to dance to the song. Moments later, Scott was arrested and charged with lewd and lascivious behavior in the presence of minors, and her two children were placed in foster homes for two days. Two neighbors peering in through the vertical blinds of Scott's third-floor apartment thought she was dancing nude. She said she was wearing a brown towel. Charges were later dropped, and Scott sued the police.

Palm Beach Post, May 14, 1989; *Orlando Sentinel*, December 31, 1989

Damien Xaros, a 23-year-old St. Lucie County man who had appeared on the Jerry Springer daytime trash-talk show in bondage gear two and a half years earlier, was convicted of initiating a "collar-earning party" for a 15-year-old boy who wanted to be Xaros's sex slave. Jurors heard graphic details of the boy performing various "tortures" as part of a sadomasochistic ritual while six others watched. Although the boy testified that all of the acts were consensual, the law does not take that into account for minors.

Palm Beach Post, October 10, 1997

Two newlyweds boarded a flight home to Southern California in Tampa but said later they didn't remember being so drunk they yelled at a stewardess, tried to stab another passenger with a fork, and continued their honeymoon in the back of the plane. The flight made an unscheduled stop in Houston, Texas, so the two could be arrested.

Palm Beach Post, December 31, 1987

A Tallahassee man trying to arrange a blind date with another man during an obscene phone call was arrested; he had mistakenly called the Leon County Sheriff's Department.

Palm Beach Post, December 25, 1988

A computer hacker reprogrammed Southern Bell equipment to route overflow calls intended for a Delray Beach probation office to a New York phone-sex line. Callers heard a recorded voice offering them a variety of sexual narratives by pushing buttons on their touch-tone telephones.

Palm Beach Post, June 14, 1989

A Palm Beach County sheriff's deputy resigned involuntarily after superiors said he had stopped female motorists, flashed his badge, and told them to expose their breasts. The two-year veteran, in uniform and a marked car, told the motorists he was looking for a woman with a tattoo on her breast who had been abducted during a bank robbery. "He didn't ever touch them," sheriff's spokesman Bob Ferrell said. "He just looked."

Palm Beach Post, December 31, 1991

A Manatee County assistant state attorney resigned after she and another assistant prosecutor led Bradenton Beach police on a 90-mile-per-hour car chase; when stopped, she was naked from the waist down. When police asked why she was half-naked, she flashed her prosecutor's badge.

Palm Beach Post, December 25, 1988

A man who rode a bicycle through his Port St. Lucie neighborhood wearing only a camisole, bra, and panties was charged with loitering and prowling. After a neighbor called 911, the man tried to flee police, but his bike crashed, and one of the balloons in his bra burst on the pavement.

Palm Beach Post, December 29, 1993

A Pensacola-area schools employee who opposed teaching sex education in public schools, was arrested and charged with driving through neighborhoods, and distributing nude photos of himself to children ranging in age from five to 10.

Orlando Sentinel, January 1, 1989

Two months after being named Sarasota's Teacher of the Year, a high school performing arts teacher was charged with having five of his 17-year-old female students dance topless for him during a class.

Orlando Sentinel, January 1, 1989

A Boca Raton man sued Tiffany's Cabaret, saying a dancer at the Boynton Beach club began an unsolicited lap dance that ended up breaking the chair and sending the man sprawling. He said nude clubs have a responsibility to make sure chairs used in lap dances can hold the weight of two people.

Palm Beach Circuit Court Records; *Palm Beach Post*, May 16, 1987

An Orlando-area cancer research center and the local American Cancer Society chapter voted to decline a $3,500 donation for breast cancer research raised by exotic dancers from the Club Juana lounge who had conducted a benefit topless car wash. A local radio station had staged the event, dubbed "Save the Boobs." A mammography center eventually took the money.

Associated Press/Palm Beach Post, May 11, 1997

After T's Lounge, a topless bar in West Palm Beach, had been busted twice in 10 months, owner Gary Odle sponsored a "Sheriff's Bar Raid," in which dancers dressed as police officers were auctioned to customers for individual dances. Deputies said the humor wouldn't stop their raids.

Palm Beach Post, December 31, 1991

A Jacksonville car wash that police closed on November 5, 1989, claimed to be America's only nude car wash. Five nude car buffers and three customers were cited when authorities shut down the weekly $10-per-vehicle event at a carport next to the Fantasy World club.

Palm Beach Post, December 11, 1989

Competitors complained when the owner of a Broward County check-cashing service hired women to sell snacks, beer, and soft drinks topless.

Palm Beach Post, December 25, 1988

Sex appeal was the prime ingredient at an Orlando diner called the Rockola Grill for Ladies Only. Male waiters wearing beach thong briefs and cutoff T-shirts would gyrate their hips and serve hot food. Owner John Chambers said, "We are the Walt Disney World of nudity." Police were not entertained; they arrested the manager and four waiters.

Orlando Sentinel, July 11, 1991

A former Broward County assistant state attorney filed a complaint against her employers after she was fired. She claimed her supervisor terminated her for wearing short, tight skirts that he said were too suggestive and made her look "like a bimbo." Brenda Taylor later declined a six-figure offer to pose for *Playboy*.

Palm Beach Post, December 25, 1988; *Orlando Sentinel*, December 31, 1989

For 20 years, Neil Cargile, a flamboyant Palm Beach gold- and diamond-mining executive who died at 67 in August 1995, spent his days pitching his beach-renourishment dredge and his nights wearing sequined women's dresses. Cargile and his "girlfriends," all dressed in gowns, would frequent night spots on the island. He insisted he was heterosexual, and he did the cross-dressing just for fun. When he was charged with drunken driving in 1994, he qualified for a public defender after proving most of his money was locked into a mining enterprise in Guyana. He insisted the arrest was because he was wearing a red-sequined minidress. And for a profile in *New Yorker* magazine, he met the reporter for lunch at a Manhattan restaurant, dressed in a man's blazer and shirt and a microminiskirt, pantyhose, and heels.

Palm Beach Post, August 3, 1995

A former Tampa fireman who quit to get a sex change demanded her job back. Alice Stehlin, née Allen Stehlin, boasted top evaluations and pay raises when she was a he. Alice later asked the city to change all references to Allen in her personnel files. The city said that would constitute altering public records.

St. Petersburg Times, August 11, 1990

Coral Springs police, strip-searching a suspect accused of bilking three Connecticut banks of more than $80,000, found out the he was a she. Authorities said Richard Wong looked and talked like a man, identified himself that way on documents, and had a wife. "He was always dressed in a suit, wore glasses, polite — a real gentleman," said West Hartford police lieutenant Anthony Duffy.

Orlando Sentinel, December 27, 1987

Seminole County sheriff's deputies, raiding the home of a suspected drug dealer, found 50 grams of cocaine and a dresser filled with plastic bags containing women's panties. Police said the man, a car mechanic, gave cocaine as well as discounts on repairs in exchange for underwear.

Orlando Sentinel, December 31, 1989

The town manager of Highland Beach, a small community near Boca Raton, filed a federal sexual harassment complaint after the vice mayor showed up at a town commission gathering carrying a box of penis-shaped pasta and a Groucho Marx–style pair of glasses in which the nose was a penis.

Palm Beach Post, June 25, 1997

A Gainesville record store owner who advertised "Come in naked for 50 percent off" was surprised when 11 people took him up on the offer; he had to stop two more women who tried to strip at closing time.

Associated Press/*Palm Beach Post*, April 17, 1993

After a 74-year-old Largo man complained to his 54-year-old wife of 30 years he wasn't getting enough sex, the argument escalated until she shot him four times, sending him to the hospital.

Associated Press/*Palm Beach Post*, January 4, 1993

FLORIDA RELIGION

Stay away from Chicken Corner.

You're likely to find the grisly remains of sacrificed animals at a western corner of Miami-Dade County's Metro Justice Building, where the county's criminal trials take place.

The courthouse has set up a "Voodoo Squad" of janitors to find and dispose of offerings made by followers of Santeria.

The Caribbean — mostly Cuban — religion, a mix of Catholicism and African rituals, uses sacrifices of food and animals as offerings to its gods. It has an estimated 70,000 followers in South Florida.

In 1993, a Santeria sect had its day in no less a venue than the U.S. Supreme Court. Animal rights activists had argued the sacrifices amounted to animal cruelty, but the high court ruled against a 1987 ordinance by the city of Hialeah banning the rituals. It said the group was protected by the Constitution's freedom of religion.

At the courthouse, defendants leave the offerings in hopes trials will go their way.

"When you leave a hex on this street, you're asking the spirits to protect your relative in jail and when they cross the street to the court," said Rigoberto Zamora, a Santeria priest.

"Sometimes we find one chicken. Sometimes we find three or four," said Raul Guasp, a courthouse maintenance man. "It depends on who is on trial."

Sometimes it will be goat's blood, sometimes a whole goat. A dove means peace. Corn is supposed to speed up a complicated case. Cakes are meant to sweeten a judge's or prosecutor's feelings toward the defendant or help win bond reduction. Eggs make the case collapse. Black pepper keeps someone in jail.

A bailiff once found two dead lizards, their mouths wrapped shut with twine, during a break in a cocaine trial. A government informant was supposed to testify. The trussed-up lizards, or a cow's tongue tied with twine, are meant to silence a snitch.

Sometimes names of the judge, prosecutor, defendant, and others are written on pieces of paper. The papers are burned and the ashes are mixed with ground-up twigs. The powder is supposed to bring good luck and sway the jury, judge, or prosecutor in favor of the accused.

In April 1995, jumpy from the Oklahoma City federal building bombing, the squad found a paper box outside the courthouse. Police blew it up. It turned out to contain a dead white dove.

Palm Beach Post, June 12, 1993, April 10, 1995; *Miami Herald*, April 27, 1995

A family holding an all-night prayer vigil for a dead relative at a funeral home was startled when ten men burst in, began performing Santeria rituals, and kicked them out. The men put ash on the body's forehead, stuck a bottle of rum in its right hand, lit candles, then ordered the family out, and closed the doors. Moments later the men apparently got into an argument and began shooting each other. Police found furniture tipped over and blood on the walls. One man was hospitalized and six questioned.

Associated Press, October 23, 1997

In the middle of a voodoo-related murder trial, a North Palm Beach exorcist performed a ceremony in a defense attorney's office to rid an urn of an evil spirit. The man used a Bible, a rope, and an incense burner for the exorcism, which he labeled a success. The defendant, a Martin County man, was on trial for murdering his father, who he said he feared would kill him and his family. Relatives said the murdered father practiced voodoo, beat his children, and molested a stepdaughter. The family continued to fear an urn they believed held a spirit the dead man controlled. The defendant later pleaded guilty and was sentenced to seven years.

Palm Beach Post, January 5, 1991

An AIDS clinic in Belle Glade, the western Palm Beach County sugar-growing town with a large Haitian population and one of America's highest AIDS rates, employed four voodoo priests to dispense real advice because many of the patients couldn't read and believed in the priests' healing powers.

Orlando Sentinel, April 26, 1987

Sightings of holy figures:

✗ At St. Nicholas Cathedral in Tarpon Springs, parishioners claimed in 1989 to have seen drops of moisture around the halo and on the cheeks of a statue of St. Nicholas, patron saint of sailors and children.
✗ That same summer, in the same town, a local gift shop owner said she was praying at the shrine of St. Michael in her Greek Orthodox church when she looked up and saw that a painting of the Virgin Mary was weeping. Within days, seven other icons at the church were said to be weeping. Soon, thousands of people flocked to the little church, many hoping to be cured of various ailments and handicaps. The weeping was believed to be a sign of impending doom. The tears stopped flowing a

few months later, but not before thousands of visitors had made nearly $5,000 in donations and lighted about $1,600 worth of holy candles.

✗ In December 1996, a woman saw a rainbow image of the Virgin Mary in black-glass windows on a two-story building in Clearwater. The image drew as many as a half-million people. Portable toilets went up and sharp merchants sold souvenir T-shirts. A morning disk jockey offered a computer game to anyone who would throw a brick through the window.

✗ And hundreds showed up at Ida Rollins' Riviera Beach home, where Rollins claimed to see a cross in her bathroom window. Rollins said one man who came was cured of his stroke.

St. Petersburg Times, July 25, 1989
Palm Beach Post, May 18, 1994; December 25, 1996

Atheists sued to have the nine-foot "Christ of the Deep" statue removed from a site 20 feet underwater at John Pennekamp State Park in the upper Keys.

Palm Beach Post, May 28, 1990

Thieves stole a baby Jesus from a Coral Springs nativity scene and left a ransom note in children's scrawl and laced with misspellings that demanded 12 Christmas cookies and three candy canes "if you ever want to see Him again." The 18-inch figurine was returned three days later, early on Christmas Day, after the owners left a note asking its return "in the spirit of Christmas." The owners said giving in to the thieves' demands would have taught them disrespect for property.

Orlando Sentinel, December 26, 1987

Twelve students registering at Florida Southern College were pulled from line at the Methodist school and told by officials to come back after they'd cut their hair. Two who protested asked whether Jesus would have been allowed to enroll.

Palm Beach Post, December 31, 1987

The Bushnell Assembly of God got a sweepstakes notice from American Family Publishers announcing that God, of Bushnell, was a finalist for a one-million-dollar prize. "God, we've been searching for you," it said. "What an incredible fortune there would be for God! Could you imagine the looks you'd get from your neighbors? Don't just sit there, God." Pastor Bill Brack responded, "I always thought he lived here, but I didn't actually know. Now I do. He's got a P.O. box here."

Associated Press/Palm Beach Post, February 28, 1997

A 50-year-old man claiming to hear the voice of God cut off his penis with a razor in front of the Sacred Heart Catholic Church in Lake Worth, saying God had told him to offer it as a sacrifice. When rescue workers arrived at the church, they found the man talking to statues.

Palm Beach Post, April 5, 1995; *Fort Lauderdale Sun-Sentinel,* December 30, 1995

A Milton woman pleaded guilty to starving her four-year-old daughter to death over the course of a year in an effort to exorcise spirits. Authorities said the girl, who should have weighed about 45 pounds, weighed 28 pounds when she died. Police said the mother, who had a master's degree, also beat the girl. An evangelist, whose alleged revelations from God led to the girl's death, was also charged with murder. The mother said in her trial that she became involved with a charismatic sect and eventually paid about $20,000 to her mentors. She said the evangelist cast a religious trance over her, might have drugged her, and convinced her that the girl was possessed by six demonic spirits that could be expelled only through fasting and punishment.

Orlando Sentinel, March 10, April 6, 1989

A Florida State University student being attacked by a wrench-wielding man broke into a chorus of "All Hail the Power of Jesus' Name," which apparently scared her assailant and saved her life. The 24-year-old woman estimated she was hit about 15 times with the wrench, which left her with a concussion. A suspect was later arrested.

Orlando Sentinel, November 15, 1987

Oscar Oliveres, born Jewish, allegedly became Boca Raton Methodist lay preacher Dennis Oliver and bilked more than 100 ministers for about $1.4 million. Investigators dubbed the case Operation Black Sabbath.

Palm Beach Post, August 20, 1989

Prominent Christian broadcaster, right-wing evangelist, and civil rights activist George Crossley of Sanford was convicted of trying to hire a hit man to kill his mistress's estranged husband.

Orlando Sentinel, October 12, 1997
Associated Press/*Palm Beach Post*, December 14, 1997

ANIMAL LIFE

In Holiday, near New Port Richey, a paralyzed man's puppy chewed off most of his left foot. Noland Britt, 42, had lost feeling below his waist in a car accident a decade earlier and didn't know the dog was gnawing on him.

The eight-week-old stray Labrador, taken in by the family the previous week, was apparently attracted to an open sore common to paraplegics. He ate the bottom of the foot, from heel to toe, down to the bone.

Britt, who was in bed, didn't know what was happening until his wife saw blood on the dog and followed a trail back to her husband's bedroom.

"She freaked," Britt said. "She told me, and I kind of looked at it comical like."

Doctors later amputated the remnant of the foot.

"I feel sorry that they have to put the dog to sleep," Britt said, "because it was a good dog."

Miami Herald, May 18, 1991

A Tampa man who used a forged license to marry a comatose woman less than four hours before she died, then ran up nearly $20,000 on her credit cards, said his bride's dog told him to do it. Robert Meier told investigators the dog told him Constance Sewell wanted him well cared for, and it would be okay to use the cards. "I thought I had seen every way to steal, scam or con people out of money," fraud detective Ed Hancock said. Sergeant Mike Olson said he found the 90-pound mutt in the garage but was unable to communicate with it.

Associated Press, August 1, 1996

A man in Steel City, about 60 miles outside of Tallahassee, insisted he wasn't feeding dead puppies to the giant snakes at his roadside zoo. He fed them live. "That's not how they eat. They eat live animals," Romulus Scalf said. Scalf later lost his permit to keep wildlife after he was convicted of animal cruelty for feeding a live pig to a liger — a cross between a lion and a tiger.

Associated Press, July 17, 1996; August 19, 1997

Shorty, a six-month-old, 23-inch Gainesville mixed-breed pit bull, swallowed an 11-inch knife handle first. The dog weighed only 23 pounds. And Pixie, a two-month-old Brooksville English bulldog/German shepherd mix, ate a seven-inch serrated steak knife. The dog weighed just over 10 pounds. Both knives were surgically removed.

Palm Beach Post, January 30, 1989; November 27, 1991

After an eight-pound male Chihuahua in Key Largo named Rocky somehow managed to seduce a rottweiler, the giant female wound up pregnant. Its owner aborted the babies, then sued little Rocky's owner, saying he could have sold real rottweiler pups for $400 each. A judge awarded him more than $2,500.

Palm Beach Post, November 6, 1993

After Chi-Chi the pot-bellied pig got too amorous with

another kind of hog — a Harley-Davidson motorcycle — the 50-pound Key West porker became a celebrity, earning itself a lawyer and a defense fund but to no avail. Despite protests, Chi-Chi was castrated.

Associated Press/*Boca Raton News*, July 28, 1995

A pair of wild pigs that wandered off course at Jacksonville International Airport collided with a landing National Guard F-16 fighter jet rolling at 160 miles per hour. The airplane was destroyed; pilot Lt. Col. Sam Carter ejected. The pigs died. "It's a very inglorious way for a $16-million aircraft to come to an end," Carter said.

Palm Beach Post, December 25, 1988; *Orlando Sentinel*, January 1, 1989

A man was eating at a Boca Raton Italian restaurant when a monkey that had escaped its owner's purse bit the diner's ear, drawing blood, then bounded across the room and back to its owner. Sigmud Rosenbaum got a tetanus shot and an attorney; police were looking for the woman, who left right after the incident.

Palm Beach Post, November 29, 1994

A Coconut Creek woman sued the movie theater where she saw *Three Men and a Baby* with her husband, claiming a rat crawled up her arm and over her head. Her attorney, Alyson Dachelet said, "She realized as it crawled up on her head: This was not her husband."

Orlando Sentinel, December 31, 1989

A giant ray leaped from the water into a 14-foot fishing boat, nearly killing five-year-old Carlton Carroll of Tallahassee. The boy suffered a concussion and a deep head wound when the eagle ray leaped into his father's boat in the Gulf of Mexico, about a mile off St. Teresa

Beach in Franklin County. "It could have easily broken Carlton's neck or fractured his skull," Rick Carroll said.

Orlando Sentinel, July 7, 1987

A turkey vulture smashed the windshield of a helicopter flying nearly 100 miles per hour over Reedy Creek, near Walt Disney World, and struck the head of passenger Buck Cooper — a resident naturalist for a local chapter of the Audubon Society. Cooper received several stitches. "He had feathers in his beard," emergency room doctor Jerry Gibbs said. "He had bird parts embedded in his face." The dead bird was left on the floor in the backseat of the helicopter. "I look a lot worse than the bird," Cooper said. "Except that he's dead."

Orlando Sentinel, December 9, 1989

A Pensacola veterinarian was sentenced to probation after pleading no contest to charges he bit a dog's nose.

Palm Beach Post, December 31, 1987

When paramedics came to a 77-year-old New Port Richey woman's home to treat an unconscious guest, they were swarmed by hundreds of beetles attracted to the light in the open front door. The medics swatted the bugs from curtains, crunched them underfoot, and picked them out of the stricken woman's hair. The bugs even got into the ambulance. The homeowner spent hours scooping the bugs and flushing them down the toilet.

St. Petersburg Times, March 20, 1991

A one-ton Brahman bull named Gandhi broke through a wire fence and fell into the swimming pool of a Jacksonville home. Two cows followed him through a fence but didn't dive in after him. Police lassoed the cold and tired animal and tried to lead him up the steps. His owner and a veterinarian gave him a shot, but that didn't work. Finally, workers ran a strap around Gandhi and hooked him to a tow truck, which extracted him from the pool.

Associated Press/*St. Petersburg Times*, February 24, 1993

A seven-foot alligator crashed through the window of Howard Ennis' Boynton Beach living room and ran into the kitchen, where it was killed by Ennis' two terriers, Bear and Nikki.

Palm Beach Post, December 29, 1993

An alligator attracted to a concrete counterpart finally went for a swim in Jean Mouhout's pool in Wellington, near West Palm Beach. A trapper hauled off seven-foot, four-inch Bruno. "All day he's trying to make it with my stone alligator," Mouhot explained. "I say, 'That's OK.' It takes him all day to figure out she's not real."

Palm Beach Post, December 29, 1993

A seven-foot, two-inch alligator trapped in an Orlando sewer for four days was caught by a trapper who coaxed it out with a mating call.

Palm Beach Post, December 31, 1987

Authorities ordered a 76-year-old Tampa woman out of her reeking, garbage-strewn home and fumigated it, later collecting more than 1,200 dead rats inside and another 105 outside the home. Authorities said the domesticated rats were not shy of humans and were used to eating out of a dish or a bag. Neighbors said that after workers first cleaned up the house, rats poured outside, making bushes sway with their weight.

Associated Press, October 8, 1997

A 110-pound Florida black bear died soon after a commercial fisherman found it swimming more than two miles out in the Gulf of Mexico near Horseshoe Beach. "It's not unusual for bears to go into the water and splash around, but two and a quarter miles out — that's unusual," said Lt. Dewey Weaver, a spokesman for the Florida Game and Fresh Water Fish Commission. "My guess is that it got disoriented and instead of swimming back to shore, it kept swimming out to sea."

Associate Press/*St. Petersburg Times*, June 8, 1994

While sailing with his master off Sugarloaf Key, an 80-pound golden retriever named Coconut Harry was swept from the deck of a trawler in a sudden squall. Eight days later, Harry swam ashore, 15 pounds lighter, at Monkey Island, five miles from where he went overboard.

Palm Beach Post, December 30, 1996

Authorities began cracking down on turtle-egg thieves with $25,000 fines and five-year jail terms in an effort to protect the endangered animals. Police have confiscated hundreds of the eggs, considered an aphrodisiac in Caribbean cultures. Police said the eggs, which went for three-for-a-dollar earlier this century, were being sold for up to five dollars each.

Palm Beach Post, July 5, 1996

A two-inch Manhattan cockroach dethroned the defending champion from Florida at the 1988 Great American Roach Off. A 1.83-inch critter found by a Hollywood sixth-grader prompted a Florida pest controller to say, "Cockroaches are to Florida what thoroughbreds are to Kentucky," but it came in only third. In 1987, Florida was national champ with a 2.18-inch Hallandale cockroach.

Palm Beach Post, December 25, 1988

Pinellas Park resident Jeff Weber built a business of freeze-drying people's favorite pets. In his first year, his Preservation Specialties preserved a Doberman, an alligator, and various birds. Customers sent their freeze-dried loved ones to Weber for the process, which slowly removed body fluids. Weber, who charged hundreds of dollars for the work, said he hoped to expand into humans.

St. Petersburg Times, February 11, 1989

A cat in Fort White, south of Lake City, gave birth to a two-headed kitten. The animal's owner said the five-year-old Calico cat Boo Boo regularly drank water that may have been contaminated by a nearby landfill. "Each face would fight itself to feed," Wilson said. "It meowed out of both mouths." He said another animal had six legs, two tails, and no head. Neither survived, although the two-headed cat lasted three days. Another was stillborn. But four others in the litter were fine.

St. Petersburg Times, July 3, 1991

A federal agent disguised in a gorilla suit and placed in a cage helped capture Mexican zoo officials at the Opa-locka Airport. The officials were shown real gorillas, orangutans, and chimpanzees at Miami-area zoos and told they could be smuggled for a fee of $92,500. "It's risky and dangerous to use a real animal, so we had to use a willing substitute," Assistant U.S. Attorney Dan Gelber said.

Associated Press/*St. Petersburg Times*, January 27, 1993

An investigation of Discovery Island, Disney's zoological park, resulted in 16 state and federal charges against Disney and five employees. They were accused of beating vultures to death, destroying the nests of ibises and egrets, shooting at hawks, and keeping large numbers of birds in small, overheated pens with insufficient food and water.

Orlando Sentinel, December 31, 1989

A ranking of the country's most pest-infested cities by pesticide manufacturer Black Flag declared Miami had more roaches than any city in America. Jacksonville was third.

Orlando Sentinel, January 1, 1989

When retired animal trainer Gene Schuler, owner of a home for old circus animals near Gainesville, used his five-ton elephant Zeta to push-start his wife's car, assistant state attorney Terry Yawn charged Schuler with allowing Zeta to escape his custody. Yawn said he would look into shutting down the 20-acre Wild Animal Retirement Village, even though that meant destroying the animals. "This close to Christmas, Mr. Yawn is beginning to look like Ebenezer Scrooge," a *Gainesville Sun* editorial said. Yawn's boss, bowing to complaints that far worse crimes demanded the state's attention, later removed Yawn from the case.

Orlando Sentinel, December 18, 1988

Police found a severed, frozen horse's head in the trunk of an abandoned car on Interstate 275 in Tampa. "It was the first horse head I've ever come across that wasn't attached to the rest of him," officer Brian O'Connor said. Police said they didn't know if the head, stuffed in a plastic bag with its tongue cut out and wrapped around its neck, was intended for some sort of cult ritual. Not finding a big enough freezer, the officers left the head in the car and impounded the vehicle. After four days, the head had defrosted enough to land the officers in trouble for improperly handling evidence.

Associated Press/*Orlando Sentinel*, September 4, 1988

Two boa constrictors, that had apparently escaped from their owners, wound up in the following places in Broward County: A Coconut Creek woman found a six-footer in her toilet. And a Pompano Beach woman awoke to find a five-and-a-half-footer around her neck.

Calamity Calendar

Authorities stopped an air cargo shipment of 41 boxes of live boas from Colombia and found cocaine-filled condoms in one. They followed a man who'd picked up the snakes to an apartment complex. After waiting several hours, the agents got a search warrant and opened the roasting van. Inside, 202 snakes were dead; the other 110 died later. Twenty-one were stuffed with cocaine totaling 80 pounds. Tests showed smugglers jammed the drugs into the snakes' rectums, then sewed them shut. "The creativity of the smuggling community has reached an all-time low," Assistant U.S. Attorney Dan Gelber said.

Miami Herald, July 3, 1993

A trucker hauling 38 million bees from Wisconsin to South Florida to pollinate crops stopped at his mother's Sarasota home for the night. While he slept, about 775,000 of the insects escaped through a tiny hole in the truck into the neighborhood. "It's admirable for a son to visit his mother on a Sunday but not with a truckload of bees," said Lawrence Cutts, Florida's chief bee inspector.

Palm Beach Post, September 7, 1994

FLORIDA LAW

A Pensacola lawyer, who became angry when a Cordova Mall gift-wrapping booth had no Hanukkah paper, went to a Cutlery World store in the mall, bought a $417 Robin Hood sword he'd seen in the window, returned to the wrapping booth, and waved it at a security guard until two bystanders tackled him. Randall Aronson, 36, was arrested on charges of aggravated assault, disorderly conduct, and resisting arrest without violence.

Miami Herald, December 24, 1992

Three armed deputies seized a Pompano Beach lawyer by the arms, dragged her from a Broward courtroom, slammed her 100-pound frame against a wall, and handcuffed her. Her crime: wearing culottes to court. The judge considered her culottes shorts, which he bans from his courtroom. Officers charged her with resisting arrest.

Palm Beach Post, September 14, 1994

West Palm Beach attorney Richard Lubin, appointed by the court to represent a murder suspect, billed Palm Beach County $17,733.18. The tab included limousines, a doctor's

Palm Beach Post

Attorney Richard Lubin billed the county for a limo and cosmetic surgery

scale, and cosmetic surgery. Lubin tried to prove his client was insane when he beat and tortured a hitchhiker. He lost the case and the county disallowed the expenses.

Orlando Sentinel, July 13, 1988

A Broward County judge threatened to punch a defendant in the mouth and sentenced him to a year in jail for contempt of court during a shouting match punctuated with curses. As bailiffs dragged Delman Daniels off, Judge Zebedee Wright said, "Hold it. Don't carry him nowhere yet. Turn him around here because I'll come out there and bust (Daniels) in the mouth." Daniels swore again, and Wright gave him another six months in jail. Daniels cursed once again, and the judge left his bench and charged him, shouting, "You want to go in that back room with me?"

St. Petersburg Times, January 6, 1990

When a man on trial in Fort Lauderdale kept falling asleep in court, two jurors were excused after saying they couldn't be fair to a man who was sleeping.

Palm Beach Post, December 31, 1987

A Philadelphia man who called himself Sir George Gordon Meade Easby claimed ownership of Florida in 1991, saying his great-great grandfather Richard Meade loaned the United States five million dollars in 1819 to buy the state from Spain and that the state itself was collateral. Easby said he'd been rummaging through his estate trying to find the documents.

Associated Press/*Palm Beach Post*, November 25, 1991

The Walt Disney people threatened to sue three preschools in Hallandale if they did not remove colorful murals of Mickey, Minnie, Donald Duck, and Goofy from their walls. Disney said it didn't want anyone to think the daycare centers were endorsed by the company. Universal Studios Florida promptly offered to paint over the Disney characters with cartoon characters of its own: the Flintstones, Yogi Bear, and Scooby Doo.

Orlando Sentinel, December 31, 1989

A Miami woman won $600,000 in court after she claimed she became legally blind after she was hit in the head with a roll of toilet paper. Peggy Fields was struck by an unknown assailant at a Surfside supermarket and suffered a torn retina. The store said a customer must have thrown the roll.

Associated Press/*Orlando Sentinel*, March 5, 1989

A former Sarasota car salesman sued his old boss, claiming he was fired in 1985 for wearing loud, ugly sport coats.

Palm Beach Post, December 25, 1988

When Ann Victoria Moore got a court order for the bank records of her ex-husband, the order was served on Kevin Collin Moore — a Kevin Moore that was 11 years older and six inches shorter than her husband. The Sunrise man told the woman he was not her ex-spouse, as did his lawyer, a judge, and police. Undaunted, she went after half his home and barraged him with court papers that ended up costing him $1,000 in legal fees.

Fort Lauderdale Sun-Sentinel, December 31, 1995

A Pensacola taxi driver had his car repossessed with his artificial right arm still in it. Richard Benka, who lost his arm in a construction accident, wouldn't pay the last $110 on a used car in a dispute with the dealer, and the car was nabbed with the arm in the trunk. An Orlando lawyer paid the fee. Benka said he doesn't always wear the arm because it gets in the way of his driving.

Orlando Sentinel, March 16, 1989

A dog charged a Boynton Beach police officer investigating a burglary and was shot five times. The dog lived and sued the city through his owners, but a judge tossed out the case. The officer, meanwhile, was later fired for committing burglaries himself.

Fort Lauderdale Sun-Sentinel, December 31, 1995

A Jacksonville man who sued the Coors beer company, claiming he had found a dead mouse in his can of beer, was sentenced to 18 months in jail after he admitted he had jammed the rodent in the can.

Palm Beach Post, December 25, 1988

A Tampa man claimed the battery in his two-year-old's Big Bird electric toothbrush blew up in his son's face,

burning his eyes and charring the ceiling.
Associated Press/Palm Beach Post, October 26, 1991

A woman visiting her mother, a worker at a Martin County nursing home, slipped in a resident's spittle and hurt her knee and hand. She sued the home, which said it put out sand urns and a cat litter box for cigarette butts, but a woman plucked the butts to make chewing tobacco, then spit the juice on the floor.
Palm Beach Post, June 10, 1996

An inmate at Martin Correctional Institution sued a Vero Beach woman for ending their romance and not sending him money. In the handwritten lawsuit, he called the woman a "selfish, ungrateful, inconsiderate deceiver" and requested $33,100 for overdue support, emotional distress, human rights violations, and "causing a sense of hopelessness."
Palm Beach Post, December 30, 1996

A West Palm Beach tenth-grader who claimed she was stood up for the prom sued the twelfth-grade-basketball star who was supposed to be her date; she won an out-of-court settlement. The young man gave the woman a check for $81.28, covering the cost of new shoes, hair styling, flowers, and court fees.
Palm Beach Post, June 20, 1989

A prominent Miami-Dade County forensic psychiatrist who, for more than three decades, testified for the state in trials — including some of South Florida's most sizzling cases — was charged with trying to bribe a police officer to find a "hit man." Michael Gilbert said he'd plead innocent by insanity. Police said Gilbert wanted to kill the father of his former second wife's nephew; he accused the man of abuse. The ex-wife, a young model, had an expensive lifestyle including a Rolls Royce and a $1,000-a-month clothes-shopping habit. Prosecutors said Gilbert told the officer the Democratic party was spying on him through a Rolex wristwatch. The state said Gilbert was faking his insanity and offered its own expert. He was later sentenced to a year in prison.

St. Petersburg Times, February 14, 1991; *Miami Herald*, May 1, 1991

A Deerfield Beach man who admitted to fatally stabbing his wife, then attempting suicide, was sentenced to watch the film *It's a Wonderful Life*, in which suicidal Jimmy Stewart is shown how lives would have been changed had he never been born.

Palm Beach Post, December 31, 1987

A man charged with breaking into a Boca Raton home said he was temporarily insane from eating too much cotton candy. He was convicted.

Fort Lauderdale Sun-Sentinel, December 29, 1996

A Stuart man who was sentenced to death three times for murdering a woman, but who won new trials every time, went to trial a fourth time. But the trial proceedings didn't last long. A prospective juror blurted out she had sat on the jury for one of his earlier trials and had voted to convict him. The 90-member jury pool was sent home.

Miami Herald, January 9, 1990

When a Daytona Beach woman sued a bra maker, saying she got permanent black marks on her breasts, defense lawyers won the right to inspect her. An appeals court agreed the lawyers had the right to inspect the injury that sparked the suit. The woman said it was just an attempt to humiliate her into settling. The court said the exam could take only two minutes and only the area with the marks had to be exposed. The only woman on the appeals panel said the lawyers could see pictures and have a doctor examine the woman.

Orlando Sentinel, May 8, 1987

A Lauderhill man who refused to pay a $25 condominium parking fine ended up in a court battle that landed him $3,233.50 in fines and attorney's fees.

Associated Press/*Palm Beach Post,* July 2, 1989

About 30 Hillsborough County sheriff's deputies, detectives, and firefighters were asked to pluck 20 pubic hairs each in the name of justice. Police said they found a pubic hair in the hallway of a Valrico home where Robert Andrew Milford was accused of murdering a 78-year-old woman and beating her husband during a robbery, then setting their house on fire and fleeing in their van. Prosecutors said the hair was similar to Milford's, while Milford claimed one of the dozens of authorities on the scene could have left it. So the state had samples pulled from those people. It said it needed the hair, follicle and root, so it had to be yanked, not cut.

St. Petersburg Times, January 25, 1992

When Brevard County grew too fast for its small courthouse, it began holding court in branch courtrooms, including a shopping mall, auditoriums, banquet halls, and poolside motel rooms. One judge presided in what had been a funeral parlor; his juries deliberated in a room where dead had been kept in their caskets. "We received verdicts in a hurry sometimes," county judge Peter Haddad said. "And we didn't work late at night."

Miami Herald, August 27, 1990

ELIOT KLEINBERG

Palm Beach Post

Attorney General Bob Butterworth went after matzoh and toilet paper

Florida Attorney General Bob Butterworth, who would later successfully sue "Big Tobacco" and win a record $368.5-billion settlement, alleged price fixing by:

✗ The nation's leading producers of toilet paper; he claimed prices had risen 41 percent since 1989 even though the cost of wood pulp had gone down 18 percent.

✗ Matzoh makers; they were charging five dollars in New Jersey and $12.50 in Florida.

✗ Contact lens suppliers; at least 20 million people who buy disposable lenses allegedly spent $135 million more than necessary; the 20 million later became eligible for a $35 rebate under a nationwide settlement.

✗ Utilities with nuclear power plants; for 14 years, they hit nearly five million customers with a surcharge to pay for a national nuclear waste disposal site that wasn't built.

Palm Beach Post, April 17, 1997; Associated Press, May 13, 1997

GO FIGURE

In a little more than a year, 13 women said to have touched an African fertility statue became pregnant. The two wooden fertility carvings, from the Baule tribe on the Ivory Coast in western Africa, were at the Orlando "Ripley's Believe It Or Not" museum. One, a woman, holds a small baby. The man holds a sword and a mango — the weapon a symbol of power and the fruit a symbol of fertility. All 13 births were boys. Three of the women worked at the Ripley's corporate office. Three were wives of Ripley workers. Three worked for companies that made frequent deliveries to the office. Four visited the Orlando area from other Ripley offices.

Associated Press, January 16, 1996

Michael Vertucci of New York had his red flatbed truck stolen in 1983. He eventually moved to Riviera Beach. Ten years later, a Martin County towing company drove into his auto-parts yard offering to sell trucks for parts. The truck was Vertucci's. Police said it had been retitled in Florida with a fake identification number. Vertucci said he planned to use the number to play the Florida lottery.

Palm Beach Post, December 29, 1993

In 1991, while tearing down a Mississippi movie theater, workers found a wallet lost there 39 years earlier by Audrey Stevens, 55, of Fort Walton Beach. It contained her junior high school yearbook photo, pictures of old girl-friends, and her first Social Security card. When contacted, Stevens remembered what movie was playing: *The Bullfighter and the Lady.*

Associated Press/*Miami Herald*, April 6, 1991

A man, believed dead since his bloodstained car was found in 1962 in Georgia, was reunited with his family in Jacksonville in 1987 after he regained his memory. James Smith said he recalled nothing over the previous 25 years. He said he awoke in a Louisiana hospital in January 1987 and said he was 27, it was 1962, John Kennedy was president, and he was working as an encyclopedia salesman in Jacksonville. Doctors said they believed a head injury caused the amnesia. He later remembered his name and tracked down his mother in Holly Hill, near Daytona Beach.

Orlando Sentinel, February 8, 1987

Police conducting a raid found a violin left behind by burglars in a run-down apartment in Holly Hill. The instrument turned out to be a 1676 Jakob Steiner, one of only 650 made and said to be as valuable as a Stradivarius. Police believe the violin was stolen from the home of a family that owned it for five generations and that it was valued at $800,000.

Palm Beach Post, November 9, 1988

Homecoming festivities were halted and police called to Forest Hill High School in West Palm Beach after four fist-fights broke out during the girls Powder Puff football game.

Palm Beach Post, December 31, 1991

Working 40 to 60 hours a week for eight months, Stephen DePirro, 52, of Port St. Lucie created a life-size sculpture of Elvis Presley out of crushed soda cans. "I just thought, 'How about soda cans?'" the artist recalled. "But no beer cans. I wanted all mom and pop."

Palm Beach Post, December 30, 1996

A Tampa television station preempted the last two minutes of "Jeopardy" to report that a plane had crashed into a house, killing two people. The station received more than 300 complaints, so it broadcast the final two minutes of the show the next day during the noon and six o'clock news.

Orlando Sentinel, January 1, 1989

Fort Lauderdale marine police pulled a woman from the Atlantic Ocean about two miles offshore. "I'm fine," she told lifeguard Breck Ballou, "my family is here." The woman said she was in the process of adapting to ocean life and had just come up for air. Ignoring her requests to return her to the sea, police took her to Memorial Regional Hospital in Hollywood for observation.

Palm Beach Post, December 30, 1996

Fort Lauderdale bartender Steve Trotter jumped off Tampa Bay's Sunshine Skyway Bridge and rappeled down San Francisco's Golden Gate Bridge. But when he went over Niagara Falls in a barrel — for the second time — he got busted and had to pay $9,000 in legal bills and fines. Six months later, back home and bolstered by a few beers, he climbed a ficus tree and fell 25 feet, breaking bones in his neck, back, and pelvis.

Fort Lauderdale Sun-Sentinel, December 31, 1995

TIMING IS EVERYTHING

A nine-year-old boy from Montora Ranch Estates, about 14 miles southwest of Clewiston, was bitten by a pygmy rattlesnake and was taken to Hendry Memorial Hospital, then to a hospital in Miami. While he was there, a tornado leveled his family's home.

Palm Beach Post, September 17, 1993

While hundreds braved death on the high seas in rickety rafts to get from Cuba to Miami, four Cuban refugees snuck aboard a luxury cruise ship at Grand Cayman and pretended to be paying passengers for four days. The four said they walked the decks of the *Majesty of the Seas* by night and slept in the movie theater by day.

Palm Beach Post, July 13, 1993

When Arthur Janis of the Century Village retirement community in West Palm Beach died, another Arthur Janis in Century Village stopped getting his Social Security checks. A few years later, Dorothy Janis, the wife of the deceased Arthur Janis, also died; the wife of the second Arthur Janis, who is also a Dorothy Janis, started hearing from the dead Dorothy Janis' creditors.

Palm Beach Post, December 2, 1993

While police frantically searched for her, 17-year-old Stacy Powell of Wauchula spent 21 hours trapped inside Hardee High School. The girl stopped at the school on a Saturday to use a phone, then walked to a restroom. A teacher giving a test then locked the school without checking inside. By midnight, authorities had issued a national bulletin. Someone finally heard her around mid-morning the next day.

Orlando Sentinel, March 15, 1989

Key West Commissioner Harry Powell suffered a broken collarbone when he was struck by a car as he rode his motorcycle home from a hearing on a proposed moped helmet law — one he opposed. He was wearing a helmet when the accident occurred. Powell would be arrested three years later for strapping a bomb to himself and threatening to blow up a navy construction project unless it was stopped. That got him two years in prison.

Miami Herald, May 16, 1991; *Palm Beach Post*, May 19, July 18, 1994

A maintenance worker at a Lake Worth apartment complex who spent two and a half hours with his arm stuck in a drain pipe said later he had reached into the drain to retrieve a lost nut.

Palm Beach Post, January 9, 1993

An antique dealer bought a desk at a St. Petersburg garage sale for $20. It turned out to be a rare antique worth up to $50,000 at auction.

St. Petersburg Times, December 7, 1989

In a seven-month span, a Tampa home caught fire, was struck by lightning, and finally caught fire a second time — this time burning to the ground. After the first fire, the owner's neighbor, a self-proclaimed clairvoyant, had told her that the home was hexed and advised her to move. "The house seems jinxed," fire captain Bill Wade said after the home was destroyed. "Maybe there's a poltergeist or an old Indian burial ground."

St. Petersburg Times, October 26, 1995

A nine-year-old Central Florida boy sitting in his dining room was struck in the back of the neck by a lightning bolt and knocked cold. Brian Grace of Lady Lake walked out of a hospital two days later. "As a rule, 999,999 times out of a million that wouldn't happen," National Weather Service meteorologist Bob Osborne said. "That's what you're supposed to do — get inside. It's just one of those freak things."

Orlando Sentinel, May 31, 1989

DUMB LUCK

A 30-year-old dancer at the Mons Venus, a nude club in Tampa, narrowly escaped death when her silicone breast implant deflected a bullet fired by a 75-year-old ex-lover. "It must have been like a bulletproof implant," Dora Oberling theorized from her hospital bed.

Palm Beach Post, December 19, 1993

A man shot Richard Daniel of Fort Pierce, but the bullets bounced harmlessly off his dentures. Daniel stabbed the shooter, who recovered. Daniel wore the dentures to his attacker's trial. Three years later, Daniel shot and killed a robber in his front yard.

Palm Beach Post, February 28, 1997

When a Riverview man was shot in the face, the bullet tore his lip and smashed into the gum portion of his dentures. The man said he spit out the bullet and drove to a hospital. "I'm alive today because of my false teeth," Charles Alexander Hinkle said as he held up his shattered dentures.

Associated Press/*Palm Beach Post,* August 26, 1990

A 10-month-old baby who was struck by a bullet during a home invasion in Tampa was, apparently, saved by her extra-thick diaper. Police found a hole the size of a nickel in the seat of the diaper worn by Brandi Ford.

Associated Press/*Miami Herald*, December 19, 1988

In Destin, a two-year-old Mississippi boy who fell from the seventh-story balcony of his family's vacation condominium onto an asphalt parking lot suffered only a few bruises and scrapes. A deputy said any fall from four floors or higher is usually fatal. Emergency workers said the tot's diaper exploded on impact.

Associated Press/*Palm Beach Post*, August 10, 1993

Three Daytona Beach seventh-graders were struck by a falling 7,620-volt electrical wire, but they escaped serious injury because a safety feature cut off the current when the line snapped. The three were coming home from a thirteenth birthday party for one of them. If a live line of that voltage had hit the three girls, they would have been killed instantly, a power company supervisor said.

Orlando Sentinel, February 3, 1987

As Victor Brancaccio walked down a Port St. Lucie street in 1993, a 78-year-old woman criticized the profane rap song he was singing. Brancaccio beat the woman to death. His parents, owners of a popular pizza restaurant, sold their home to pay his legal bills but worried it wouldn't be enough. Then they won $2.4 million in the Florida lottery. Their son was later convicted and sentenced to a life term.

Palm Beach Post, October 14, 1995

In 1987, Joe Crowley won three million dollars in the Ohio lottery. He moved to Florida and kept playing there.

In December 1993, he became the first person ever to win the Florida lottery after winning another state's jackpot. Just winning the Florida lottery is about a 14-million-to-one shot. This time, the payoff was $20 million. Sixty-six-year-old Crowley guessed he spent about $250 a week on scratch-off tickets, Cash 3, Fantasy 5, and Lotto.

Palm Beach Post, December 30, 1993

Karol and Margaret Majoros went to a Cumberland Farms store near Orlando and paid for eight lottery tickets. But the clerk accidentally printed three more. Majoros bought them, too. One had the winning numbers and was worth $14.2 million.

Palm Beach Post, June 14, 1991

Handy and Jeanette Flemming of Moultrie, Georgia, bought a lottery ticket at a North Florida liquor store. Lightning knocked out power as they bought the ticket; the computer registered the number but didn't print the ticket. The power returned three minutes later and the clerk fed the play slips through again. The result: the Flemmings unknowingly had two of the four winning draws and half of the $7.36-million jackpot.

Palm Beach Post, July 27, 1990

Eustis bartender Tammy Bohman got her usual tip from one of her regular customers: four Florida lottery scratch-off tickets. One was for a free ticket; she traded it for another that paid off $10,000.

Orlando Sentinel, October 21, 1989

DUMB PEOPLE

An employee at a Builders Square in West Palm Beach wanted to prove to a coworker that mineral spirits don't burn. He poured some liquid on the floor and lit it. Fire damage to the building was about one million dollars; corporate officials who'd planned to phase out the store anyway said they would not reopen it. About 90 people lost their jobs, including the employee who started the fire.

Palm Beach Post, December 22, 1993

While repairing his car, Claude Fleury of Lake Worth tossed some spark plugs into a pot and put it on the stove to cook off the carbon. Then he left for lunch. A neighbor heard the explosion.

Palm Beach Post, October 3, 1992

A New Port Richey man teaching his friend how to use a shotgun decided he was far enough away, then said, "I know what I'm doing. Go ahead and shoot." The man, who had walked off only half the required safe distance, was treated for birdshot wounds.

Palm Beach Post, December 31, 1987

A veteran Miami Beach firefighter extended the 90-foot-ladder of a city fire truck without using stabilizer jacks; the $500,000 truck tipped over and crashed onto the firefighter's personal pickup.

Orlando Sentinel, January 1, 1989

A 23-year-old Taiwanese student studying at Florida Atlantic University handed a note to a flight attendant on a Washington D.C.–to–Fort Lauderdale Continental Airlines flight. It read, "Yes, the thing you fear the most is happening right now. Yes, I do have a bomb." Fernando Chen was arrested when the plane landed. "I said it's a joke, and I told them beforehand so there would be no mistakes," he said. He explained he was a photographer for the FAU newspaper and just wanted to request a picture of himself and the flight crew in a unique way.

Orlando Sentinel, January 1, 1989

Four officers with drawn guns confronted the black caretaker of a sailboat moored at a Fort Lauderdale marina after someone called to say a black man was removing items from the boat. After the incident, the man posted a sign on the boat reading, "Black Man On Board."

Orlando Sentinel, December 31, 1989

A night watchman at the Fort Lauderdale Museum of Art called rescue workers to revive a woman he found sitting in the lobby and not breathing. After racing downtown with their emergency equipment, firefighters found the woman was, in fact, a work by sculptor Duane Hanson, whose work was on display.

Palm Beach Post, December 31, 1991

During a meeting with bureau reporters, *Tampa Tribune*

publisher Richard F. "Red" Pittman referred to a black activist who had recently been in the news as "that nigger." He later apologized, saying it was "a slip of the lip" and added, "It was not intended as a racial slur." J. Stewart Bryan, Pittman's boss and the chief operating officer of Media General Inc., which owns the *Tribune*, said: "I really don't see what all the fuss is about. I'm sure I have used the word more than once. . . . It does not connote a character flaw that someone would use a word that was common parlance when Mr. Pittman was growing up."

Orlando Sentinel, December 31, 1989

Houston Astros pitcher Bob Knepper, after playing in a spring-training game in Kissimmee officiated by one of baseball's first female umpires, said, "There are certain things a woman shouldn't be, and an umpire is one of them. It's a physical thing. God created women to be feminine. I don't think they should be competing with men." He dug his hole deeper by adding, "It has nothing to do with her ability. I don't think women should be in any position of leadership. I don't think they should be presidents or politicians. I think women are created not in an inferior position but in a role of submission to men." He wasn't done: "You can be a woman umpire if you want, but that doesn't mean it's right. You can be a homosexual if you want, but that doesn't mean that's right either."

Orlando Sentinel, January 1, 1989

In September 1995, South Florida television stations owned by NBC and CBS swapped channel positions as part of a related swap in Philadelphia. Everything that had been seen on Channel 6 would now appear on Channel 4; what had been on 4 would now be seen on 6. Both stations instituted toll-free hot lines for people who were confused by this.

WTVJ-TV, WFOR-TV

DUMB CRIMINALS

Two men charged with murder after they killed a Boynton Beach jewelry store owner in a botched heist told police they needed the money for the police academy. "He actually said, 'I guess I can't be a police officer now,'" detective Ray Schilke said of one.

Palm Beach Post, December 7, 1996

A man took a taxi to a Boynton Beach bank, waited impatiently for five minutes for the bank to open, removed his hat and sunglasses, robbed the bank in full view of a surveillance camera, took the cab back to his hotel then announced to another guest he'd come into money and was upgrading to a nearby Ramada Inn. A police check of cabs tracked down the robber, who had also left his holdup note in the taxi's backseat. "He was kind of a dumb robber," cabbie John Fineo said.

Palm Beach Post, October 30, 1997

A man who was later arrested said "please" and "thank you" and had no weapon when he slipped a teller at a Dania bank a note reading in part, "I'm new at this."

Palm Beach Post, December 31, 1987

Police said a Connecticut man flew to Miami three times to hold up the same tellers at the same bank, wearing the same clothes and using the same BB gun.

Orlando Sentinel, July 18, 1987

A Fort Pierce man in a wheelchair allegedly tried to rob a car. Witnesses said two men pushed the man's chair to a car where he pulled a gun, grabbed the steering wheel, and demanded money. The driver sped off, dragging the wheelchair two blocks; the robber then let go and fell onto some grass.

Palm Beach Post, December 31, 1991

Police in Naples charged a man with stealing more than $40 worth of razor blades from a Wal-Mart. He reportedly outran a security officer but was arrested when he returned a few minutes later and demanded a refund.

News of the Weird/Bloomington (Ind.) *Voice*, December 1996

Two brothers were convicted of kidnapping a 10-year-old Naples girl, the great-great-granddaughter of the head of the Mueller noodle empire; among the evidence was a picture of the girl sent with a $1.5-million ransom note covered with their fingerprints.

Palm Beach Post, December 31, 1987

State prison officials received an authentic-looking court order to release a convicted forger in his first year of a 15-year term. The order had an official stamp and the apparent signature of a Jacksonville judge. But they realized it was fake when several words were misspelled, including "fourth," "defense," and the judge's name.

Orlando Sentinel, December 31, 1989

The former live-in caretaker of a 71-year-old paraplegic widow pleaded guilty to stealing $800,000 from the Bartow woman. The caretaker said she donated most of the money to a television evangelist.

Palm Beach Post, July 13, 1989

Deputies in Fort Myers dialed the number to a stolen pager; the alleged robber then called them back and ended up in jail.

Associated Press/*Orlando Sentinel*, February 25, 1994

KEYSTONE COPS

After people across America saw a photograph of Port St. Lucie police officer Charles Lamm on the hood of his car, pointing a handgun at a six-foot alligator that was blocking traffic, it was reported that Lamm had retired from the New York police department on disability three years earlier and was getting almost $30,000 a year in benefits — almost his total Port St. Lucie salary. Port St. Lucie police said New York's disability threshold was too low, and they had no problem hiring Lamm, who had suffered hearing loss in his right ear.

Palm Beach Post, November 14, 1994

If you dial the three-man police department in Carrabelle, a Gulf Coast town with a population of 1,800, your call will ring simultaneously in three places: a hallway at Town Hall, the desk of the town's secretary, and a telephone booth out on Highway 98. That last one's the police station. The curious come by all the time to see what is reportedly the world's smallest police headquarters. Some even stop at a nearby shop to buy a T-shirt depicting the oddity. Officers will answer if they're passing by and hear the phone ring or are told on the two-way to take a call.

The beige telephone has no dial, so calls only come in.

Palm Beach Post, October 17, 1993

Leon County officers investigating a woman's disappearance conducted a "meticulous" search of her home, collected evidence, and videotaped the residence, but they missed her beaten and strangled body under her bed. It wasn't discovered until three days later.

Orlando Sentinel, January 1, 1989

Two Miami officers who had been designated to lecture on the evils of drugs were arrested on cocaine charges.

Palm Beach Post, December 31, 1987

After a car chase, two car accidents, and a gun battle near Miami International Airport, police officers disguised as drug dealers arrested drug dealers disguised as police officers.

Orlando Sentinel, January 1, 1989

Martin County deputies testified under oath that they had not made three suspected drug dealers stand in anthills or sit in a patrol car with the heater running during an I-95 arrest.

Palm Beach Post, December 31, 1991

The Metro-Dade Bomb Squad, using unclaimed Eastern Airlines luggage to train bomb-sniffing dogs, left a stick of dynamite in a suitcase belonging to a couple who found the explosives when they reclaimed their bag.

Orlando Sentinel, January 1, 1989

Two Orlando officers who wore Ronald Reagan masks during a visit by Vice President George Bush were given written reprimands.

Palm Beach Post, December 31, 1987

The Broward County sheriff's department took to manufacturing its own crack cocaine rocks for use in sting operations after it said it couldn't get enough crack on the street.

Orlando Sentinel, December 31, 1989

Three Miami homicide detectives were suspended after a burp by one of them during an investigation was accidentally broadcast on a police channel, and none of the three would own up to it. The one who did it was eventually tracked down by his radio log.

Palm Beach Post, December 25, 1988

A plumber in Miami-Dade County's Liberty City neighborhood was arrested at a Winn-Dixie store for eating a handful of white seedless grapes out of a $1.65 package in his cart. Charges were eventually dropped.

Orlando Sentinel, January 1, 1989

West Palm Beach Mayor Jeff Koons was arrested, handcuffed, and taken to jail in August 1991 after a warrant was issued against him for missing a court date over a three-year-old leash law violation. Koons was released on bond and later ordered to pay $50 to the Animal Rescue League.

Palm Beach Post, December 31, 1991

Deputies in Gainesville planted a motorcycle to try to catch an elusive thief. They watched it for 17 days. An officer took a two-minute restroom break and returned to find the bike gone.

News of the Weird

FLORIDA: LAND OF CRIME

A dishwasher was accused of taking 370 dirty diapers from St. Petersburg–area porches and at least 1,500 from a diaper pickup service. The man was wearing a disposable diaper when police arrested him at his home, where they found the 370 neatly folded and cleaned diapers. Police said they found an address list of mothers he picked from newspaper birth announcements and surveyed about diaper use.

Orlando Sentinel, January 26, 1987

A 19-year-old robbery suspect freed without bail walked out of a Miami court hearing and promptly stole a new van.

Palm Beach Post, December 25, 1988

A six-foot-two, 475-pound Miami-Dade County man was arrested at the Tallahassee airport after police found three-fourths of a pound of crack cocaine between the fleshy, pouchlike folds of his belly. Police on antidrug patrol approached the man because he fit a profile of drug carriers, a spokesman said. Officials found nothing, but when a drug-sniffing dog was adamant, an officer lifted a fold of the man's abdomen and found the drugs. "He had to reach way in to get it out," said Ernie Stoll, the dog's handler. "It was all compressed."

Miami Herald, June 26, 1991

Officials estimated that nearly half the heroin seized in South Florida in 1992 arrived at Miami International Airport in thumb-sized pellets in smugglers' intestinal tracts.

Associated Press/Orlando Sentinel, May 10, 1993

A Pahokee man told West Palm Beach police he traveled to and from more than 30 burglaries on city buses. The man said he was a crack cocaine addict who sold his loot almost immediately. "We appreciate his trying to conserve fuel," police sergeant John English said.

Palm Beach Post, December 31, 1991

Thirty-year-old Premnath Hardeo was charged with petty theft after confessing he had been stealing and eating rare goldfish from a condominium pond. The man told police that the 12-inch koi were a delicacy in his native Sri Lanka.

Orlando Sentinel, December 31, 1991

A video camera caught a shopper gulping a diamond ring, so authorities put her in jail and waited until she passed it. Police said the woman had tried on the .96-carat ring at a Tampa department store's jewelry counter.

Palm Beach Post, March 27, 1993

A man trying to pass a stolen check at a Jacksonville Winn-Dixie store ate the check before police could stop him. He was arrested anyway, charged with two counts of forgery, resisting arrest with violence, and tampering with evidence.

Orlando Sentinel, January 30, 1987

Police said South Florida's Biting Bandit bit more than a dozen victims, chewing off a piece of one man's ear and another one's finger.

Palm Beach Post, January 30, 1990

A former employee demanding his final paycheck bit off his supervisor's right index finger during a scuffle. Officers later were unable to find the finger.

Orlando Sentinel, December 6, 1987

Apparently random attacks by two men with blowgun-type darts left three Tampa men ill; investigators said the darts might have been tipped with poison. Two men were struck about 15 minutes apart and a third 10 days later. The darts were about three inches long and fashioned from a sewing needle attached to a plastic tube and topped with cotton.

Palm Beach Post, September 15, 1989

At a West Palm Beach theater, one woman told another three times to keep quiet. The noisy patron turned and sprayed her critic's eyes and face with Mace then fled the theater. The victim was treated by paramedics. The general manager said the incident was the first at his theater, which he said "vigorously" enforces a "silence is golden" policy. The film: *Fire in the Sky*, a tale of alien abduction.

Palm Beach Post, April 3, 1993

Authorities said "Blockhouse Bandit" Robert Litchfield hit

Boca Raton–area banks, taking tellers' driver licenses and threatening to track them down and kill them if they cooperated with police. After a second prison break, Litchfield tried to get a plastic surgeon to make him look like actor Robert De Niro.

Palm Beach Post, August 20, 1989

A Miami judge sentenced a homeless man to 40 years in prison for stealing 22 rolls of toilet paper. The judge insisted she was sentencing Henry Stepney for that and his 51 prior arrests.

Palm Beach Post, September 29, 1996

Miami storekeeper Prentice Rasheed, fed up with continued break-ins, rigged a booby-trap grate that electrocuted a would-be burglar. Rasheed was cleared of wrongdoing and said he planned to market the device.

Palm Beach Post, December 31, 1987

A Tampa convenience store manager, fed up with pimps, prostitutes, and other loiterers, began piping Muzak through outside speakers.

Tampa Tribune, September 17, 1991

A convicted drug dealer forced by court order to wear a monitoring instrument while under house arrest pawned the $1,700 device for five dollars at a Fort Lauderdale pawn shop, saying it was an answering machine.

Fort Lauderdale Sun-Sentinel, December 31, 1995

Authorities investigated a statewide network of 70 to 100 transvestites who conducted smash-and-grab robberies of boutiques from Miami to Jacksonville, shattering storefront windows and cleaning out clothes. Authorities said they believed a loosely organized band was behind the crimes; one raid in Lake Park, near West Palm Beach, uncovered 1,500 cocktail dresses.

Palm Beach Post, August 10, 1992

West Palm Beach police found two burglars unknowingly hitting the same place. Officers responding to a burglar alarm at Liberty Scrap Metal found a man scaling a fence on the south side and another fleeing from the west side. The first man said he was stealing copper pipe, the other aluminum cans.

Palm Beach Post, December 29, 1993

After a passenger couldn't come up with the $42 cab fare from Fort Lauderdale to Boca Raton's Mizner Park shopping and entertainment complex, driver Edward Blagden locked him in the trunk. "I put him in the trunk for safekeeping and that wasn't legal. I didn't know that," Blagden explained. There was an outrage when no charges were filed against the passenger but Blagden was charged with false imprisonment; the charge was later dropped.

Palm Beach Post, March 4, December 29, 1993

A woman waiting at a red light in Palm Beach County was accosted by a would-be carjacker who ordered her from her car. "You're crazy. This car's paid for," the woman said; she then hit him on the head with her Club steering wheel lock, ran the red light, and escaped.

Palm Beach Post, May 18, 1993

An 18-year-old Tampa student said she was abducted at gunpoint by an Elvis Presley impersonator who made her drive 10 hours to the Birmingham, Alabama, airport, then fled. "He might have looked like Elvis," University of South Florida freshman Wendy Durgan said, "but he sure didn't sing like him."

St. Petersburg Times, November 17, 1988

A carjacker made a fatal mistake when he forced businessman Paul Brite into the trunk of his Lexus at a Coral Springs car wash and drove off with the man's car. Fearing Brite had a cellular phone, the thief stopped and popped the trunk. Brite came out with the two guns he kept stored there and ordered the thief to the ground. He fired two warning shots and, when his assailant reached in his pocket, shot once, fatally injuring the man. An accomplice who was following in another car then tried to run Brite down but fled when Brite fired at him; the second man was later caught.

Associated Press/Palm Beach Post, July 25, 1995

A Jacksonville man told police he was kidnapped as he made a bank deposit, painted black, and eventually kicked from his moving truck 155 miles away in Tifton, Georgia. The man was found unconscious in a ditch with his face spray-painted black — the paint drying his eyelids over his eyes and paint in his mouth, nose, and ears. Police said the abductor stole about $13,000.

St. Petersburg Times, July 13, 1989

A woman charged with robbing several Palm Beach County Pizza Huts turned out to be a driver for Domino's Pizza.

Fort Lauderdale Sun-Sentinel, July 13, 1995

A newspaper delivery man called police from a phone booth after witnessing a burglary and was held up by an

armed robber as the dispatcher listened. A man demanded the victim's wallet then sped away in a car. By the time
police arrived, the robber was gone.

Orlando Sentinel, April 6, 1989

The Citrus County Commission approved a law requiring
mystics to register with the county and provide background and references. Violators could be fined up to
$500 and spend up to 60 days in jail. The move came
after a spiritualist accused of fraud was barred from the
county for six months. Former clients said she took up to
$15,000 per case to lift curses but never did.

   Broward County also reported receiving dozens of complaints that soothsayers took thousands of dollars from
people to chase demons or bring good luck. "I look at the
complaints we get as just the tip of the iceberg," said Kent
Neal, prosecutor in charge of the state attorney's
Economic Crime Unit in Fort Lauderdale. "Often people
who are victims are too embarrassed to file a complaint."
One of those arrested allegedly promised one woman she
could chase away evil spirits by burying $26,000 of the
woman's money in the Egyptian sands.

St. Petersburg Times, December 4, 1989; August 26, 1992

Authorities in Hillsborough County said a Lakeland "spiritual adviser" put satanic hexes on his landlord and on a
woman who refused his advances. Deputies found more
than 100 voodoo dolls, a red cloth pouch with more than
100 small, square slips of paper with bizarre drawings
and messages, and 23 small strips of notebook paper
rolled tightly into tiny squares that were apparently curses. Three blood-splattered satanic messages were stuffed
into the mouth of a pig's head left on the grave of a nine-
year-old girl. Deputies said they don't believe the man
knew the girl but intended for the landlord and the disin-
terested woman to contract whatever disease killed the

young girl. The girl's family had the grave reblessed.

St. Petersburg Times, April 22, 1995

Authorities said Anthony "Puppy Eyes" Lamonica had at least 11 wives and swindled most of them by selling bogus casino shares. Lamonica took two million dollars alone from one wife and her friends. "He just walked out of the door one morning, a weekday, and said he'd be back for dinner, and he never came back," one wife said. "I hope he gets AIDS."

Palm Beach Post, August 20, 1989

Tampa newlyweds Laurette and Richard Brunson, both 50 years old, had been married only a couple of hours when they had their first fight — at the wedding reception. The bride threw a plate of macaroni salad at the groom, who responded by whipping out a .22-caliber handgun and shooting her in the abdomen. She survived.

Palm Beach Post, December 31, 1992

Thieves in the Pasco County town of Holiday stole 300 rubber ducks being stored for an American Cancer Society charity race. "How could anybody be so low as to steal from the American Cancer Society, and especially something so stupid as ducks?" Program Coordinator Laura Dolby said. The society said it had 4,000 more ducks.

Associated Press/*Orlando Sentinel*, August 18, 1989

An 11-year-old boy set fire to Southboro Elementary School in West Palm Beach in hopes he would be transferred to the elementary school of his sweetheart. The fire did one million dollars worth of damage to the school. The boy was suspended, and his girlfriend broke up with him when she found out.

Palm Beach Post, February 15, 1989

Miami News

James Gisclair "adopted" a welfare family

Boca Raton businessman James Gisclair announced on NBC's "Today" show that he was "adopting" welfare mom Anita Hunter and her five children and rescuing them from poverty in downtown Miami's Overtown neighborhood. The next day, it was revealed that Gisclair had failed to pay a $1.5-million civil judgment against him, faced charges of criminal fraud, and had sworn in court that his six businesses were worthless. Gisclair did move Hunter and her family to Boca Raton, but he didn't find her a job. It turned out Gisclair had been convicted the previous year of bank fraud and sentenced to two years in prison.

Palm Beach Post, June 15, 1994

On a day when substantial snow fell on Pensacola for the first time in a decade, three grinches in a pickup stole a six-year-old's snowman, threw it in the back of their truck along with at least a dozen more, and fled.

Associated Press/*Miami Herald*, March 16, 1993

PRISON BLUES

A man serving a life sentence for arranging the contract murder of his wife, a former West Palm Beach assistant city manager, planned an ambitious helicopter escape from a state prison in Zephyrhills. Robert Spearman also planned to use a hand grenade to kill his prosecutor.

Prison officials uncovered the plot. Two undercover agents posed as pilots and received a down payment to fly Spearman out. They were to land in the prison yard, loaded with automatic weapons, and take Spearman to a nearby airport where they would board a stolen plane. Spearman hanged himself in prison about a week after the plot was exposed.

Palm Beach Post, March 25, 1989

Frank Valdes, on death row for murdering a prison guard during an escape attempt, married Wanda Eads, 14 years his senior, in prison. The two met when Valdes and Eads' son were in the same juvenile facility. It took four years to get permission. Four months after the marriage, Valdes filed for divorce, but he dropped the idea a few months after that.

Palm Beach Post, February 24, 1991; December 22, 1994

Two fiery executions raised debate about the use of Florida's electric chair, used for three-fourths of a century.

In 1990, prison officials ordered an extensive review after convicted murderer Jessie Tafero's head caught fire during his execution, sending flames and smoke shooting from his head.

For four minutes, Tafero continued to breathe and slowly nod his head as his executioners repeatedly turned the current on and off. Each time they turned the switch back on, flames shot out and smoke rose from underneath the black mask covering his face. Tafero, condemned for killing two police officers in Broward County, was finally pronounced dead.

Florida Department of Corrections

Jesse Tafero's head caught fire
in the electric chair

A prison spokesman insisted Tafero was dead with the first jolt and the breathing was involuntary reflex.

In 1997, as a jolt passed through Pedro Medina's body, flames ignited his death mask. Moments later, the smell of burning flesh enveloped the room. "It was gruesome. Absolutely gruesome," said the Reverend Glenn Dickson, Medina's pastor. Attorney General Bob Butterworth said, "People who wish to commit murder better not do it in the state of Florida because we may have a problem with our electric chair."

Miami Herald, May 5, 1990; Palm Beach Post, March 26, 1997

When 28-year-old Liace Pierre was released from the St. Lucie County Jail after serving a sentence for aggravated assault, authorities gave him a new set of clothes. "Halfway down Orange Avenue he decided he didn't like them any more and just took them off," Capt. Dennis Nickel said. "We're not sure why." Pierre was arrested again.

Palm Beach Post, December 31, 1991

A 35-year-old man asked Palatka police to arrest him so he could get a decent meal. When they refused, he threw bricks through three windows at the Putnam County Courthouse and had a filling meal in his jail cell.

Palm Beach Post, December 25, 1988

Two Florida prisons announced that incorrigible prisoners would be disciplined by being fed "confinement loaf," an unappetizing concoction that looked like meat loaf but was made of nonfat dry milk, cubed whole wheat toast, grated cheddar cheese, dehydrated potato flakes, carrots, spinach, raisins, navy beans, vegetable oil, and tomato paste.

Orlando Sentinel, January 1, 1989

BellSouth employees working on computer software for the pay phones at the St. Lucie County Jail in June accidentally made it possible for inmates to charge long-distance calls to any number between Boca Raton and northern Broward County.

Palm Beach Post, December 30, 1996

After a Seminole County Jail guard asked for a week of administrative leave for his mother's funeral in Arizona, the jail chief was surprised three months later when the "dead" woman called looking for her son. The guard then admitted he had lied and offered to quit, but the sheriff, instead, fired him and deducted the leave pay from his final paycheck.

Orlando Sentinel, November 30, 1988

DEATH

Fans at a Delray Beach National Little League game paused in silence to honor Thomas Johnson, the city's beloved "Peanut Man." But Johnson wasn't dead. Organizers said they'd heard second hand that he'd died and did the moment of silence on the spur of the moment. Johnson, famed for bicycling down city streets with bags of nuts around his neck and waist, died for good about a year later. He was 84.

Palm Beach Post, May 22, 1994

North Miami planned its 1988 Veterans Day celebration around a memorial for its last World War I veteran, Elmer Smith — city officials were told he had died that summer. But Smith, 88, turned out to be alive. The city went ahead and made him the honored guest, but he declined to give a speech: "What's a dead man to say?"

Orlando Sentinel, January 1, 1989

A golfer who suffered a fatal heart attack lay dead for three hours on the sixteenth green of a Winter Haven course while police argued over which funeral home to call. Donald DeGreve, 65, died while putting at the city-owned Willowbrook Golf Course with about 40 of his neighbors from Swiss Village Mobile Home Park. As his body lay covered by a sheet, his three partners went to find his widow, but the rest of the group played through.

Associated Press/Fort Lauderdale Sun-Sentinel, November 16, 1991

When a 67-year-old Lake Worth resident died of a heart attack as he drove through John Prince Park, his car rolled through a fence and hit a tree. A passer-by saw the accident and the body in the car and called police from a pay phone. But before authorities could arrive, someone pulled the body from the car, took the personal possessions from the pockets, and stole the car.

Palm Beach Post, December 31, 1992

A 270-pound West Palm Beach woman was charged with manslaughter after she fell on her 140-pound boyfriend and crushed him. Thirty-nine-year-old Viola Thompson told police she fell on 48-year-old Augustus Grant during a fight after they had been drinking. She said she later awakened to find Grant unconscious, face down on the bed, and bleeding from his nose.

Palm Beach Post, May 11, 1995

Worker Ramon José Rodriguez was struck and killed by a portable toilet blown by a gust of wind off the fourth floor of a Miami building under construction. A local meteorologist said winds that high up could have been about 30 miles per hour at the time.

St. Petersburg Times, December 24, 1988

Frank Nelson Seton, a 24-year-old Orange County deputy, fell 40 feet to his death while hanging from a helicopter during a search for two shooting suspects.

Associated Press/*Miami Herald*, January 5, 1989

A 16-year-old in a dropout prevention class at Tampa's Adams Junior High died after playing a game called "B" in which players take turns punching each other in the chest. Victor Guzman reportedly asked one of the other three, "Is that as hard as you can hit?" then collapsed.

Associated Press/*Fort Lauderdale Sun-Sentinel*, February 25, 1993

A 62-year-old man who was complaining at a West Palm Beach City Council budget hearing suddenly dropped dead at the podium from an apparent heart attack. James E. Grove died just as he finished speaking against a new tax rate and the way his municipal tax dollars were being spent. "He was a great man," said his son, Elliott. "I think he was really caring about taxes and stuff. He must have just got upset."

Palm Beach Post, September 19, 1989

When retired municipal worker John Webster died at 78, relatives found he had glued thousands of slippers, golf balls, cigarette butts, and other discarded items to the walls of his suburban Lake Worth mobile home.

Palm Beach Post, December 31, 1994

The family of 18-year-old auto accident victim Sherri Blunder spent six days at the comatose girl's bedside, only to find out she was Heather Steverson. Steverson's family had already buried Sherri, Heather's best friend. The bodies were exhumed three months later and thumbprint records confirmed the mixup, erasing doubts that had been with the Steversons for weeks. "I'm glad it's over," Hermon Steverson said. "It's been a nightmare." Relatives said the two had the same athletic build, similar hair-styles, were only six pounds different in weight, and their faces were badly swollen after the crash.

Orlando Sentinel, September 29, 1987

When a woman went into cardiac arrest at a St. Petersburg hospital, doctors pronounced her dead and placed her in a body bag. About an hour later, when the woman's children arrived at the hospital for their final good-byes, they found her in a body bag up to her chest. Her head was lolling, and she was gasping for air. The woman died for good two months later.

St. Petersburg Times, March 1, 1992

A 67-year-old Port Orange man made arrangements to spend eternity in a $30,000 mausoleum with bulletproof windows, sitting at the wheel of his DeLorean sports car. Philip Miuccio built the tomb on a hill overlooking a runway at the Daytona Beach airport. He said he couldn't imagine being alive or dead without his prized possession. With only about 4,000 miles on it at the time, the four-and-a-half-foot high, 2,700-pound car would probably double the value of the $26,000-tomb Miuccio paid for in 1981.

Orlando Sentinel, October 31, 1987

A man in Pensacola opened a funeral home with a drive-through window, but only two families used it to display their loved ones in the Junior Funeral Home's first seven months in business. Owner Willie Junior said motorists would drive by to see who might be on display or just to see how the window worked even if a body wasn't inside. It looked similar to a drive-in bank window. Drive-through mourners could even sign a guest book on a swing-out tray.

Orlando Sentinel, February 22, 1987

Lake Worth designer Anjulina Laurie introduced "Nosferatu," a line of dresses made from satin and velvet coffin linings.

Palm Beach Post, December 1, 1994

An Indiantown minister arrived at the Port Mayaca Cemetery with a body and mourners, only to find that no grave had been dug and no cemetery employees were around to dig one. The cemetery manager later offered to sell the family a marker at cost to make up for the mistake.

Palm Beach Post, December 31, 1992

A Port St. Lucie woman found a funeral urn full of ashes abandoned outside her home. The urn had not been reported missing, police said.

Palm Beach Post, December 29, 1993

Burglars who broke into a Boynton Beach man's home left a radio, television, VCR, and watch but took the ashes of his cremated sister.

Fort Lauderdale Sun-Sentinel, June 4, 1993

MURDER MOST FOUL

Police said a man decapitated his girlfriend and then ran naked through the streets before hurling the woman's head at an officer, saying, "I killed her! She's the devil!" Veteran Miami homicide sergeant Mike Gonzalez was moved to observe, "There is no end to the bizarreness of the world."

Palm Beach Post, November 13, 1987

Police arrested a North Tampa man for murder after finding a woman's dismembered body in his freezer. The body was complete and investigators believed it had been there at least three years.

Associated Press/*Miami Herald*, March 8, 1988

At least six Brevard County teenagers saw the body of a stabbing victim for 24 hours and ignored it, even stealing items from the victim's house, before one of them finally told police. "They looked through the house and decided, 'He won't be needing any of this anymore,'" Detective George Santiago said.

Associated Press/*Palm Beach Post*, April 3, 1994

Nineteen-year-old Hillsborough County Satan worshiper Jonathan Cantero, who pleaded guilty to stabbing his mother 40 times and slitting her throat, said he made a list of things to do that day. "Go to school, leave at 11:45, pull up at mom's house, enter—greet mom, go to the bathroom, prepare knife and handkerchief, go directly to mom, when back is turned. Cover her mouth, stab until dead, cut off her left hand."

Cantero told police he hated his mother for preaching Christianity and tried to cut off her hand to show his allegiance to Satan. He also read a satanic poem that says in part, "Lord Satan, thou I had stricken this woman from the Earth, I have slain the womb from which I was born. I have ended her reign of desecration of my mind, she is no longer of me, yet only a simple serpent on a lower plane."

Orlando Sentinel, March 18, 1989

A 21-year-old Seminole County man told a Lutheran pastor a strange and powerful force had told him to control his life and destroy anyone who challenged him. Days later, police said, Sean McCollum beat his mother to death with a baseball bat. Her hands and feet were cut off, her neck fractured with a hatchet, other body parts mutilated, and her heart cut out. "There was a time bomb waiting to go off," said Rev. Frank Ledvinka, who counseled the man. He said he did not contact police following McCollum's visit because he had seen similar cases before.

Orlando Sentinel, July 15, 1997

A Port Orange woman convicted of strangling her boyfriend said she killed him accidentally during satanic rituals and kinky sex.

Orlando Sentinel, June 29, July 7, 1993

A visitor dressed in a clown's suit and mask handed a

Wellington woman balloons and a basket of red and white flowers, then shot the woman dead in front of her two teenaged sons and their friends. Police later said they believed the shooter was the girlfriend of the victim's husband, and the two conspired in the slaying, but the police didn't have enough evidence to convict them.

Palm Beach Post, May 24, 1991

An 88-year-old resident of a cramped Dade City retirement home who was fed up with his roommates went room to room bludgeoning sleeping people with his walking cane, killing two. The man killed his 90-year-old roommate and a 73-year-old woman. At least four other people were also injured in the home, which housed nine residents.

Associated Press/*Miami Herald*, January 3, 1989

A man released from a North Florida prison took a bus straight to Jacksonville to see a man about a job, talked for two hours to the man's roommate while he awaited his potential employer, then stabbed the roommate to death. Phillip Ross Winchester was supposed to have reported first to the local Salvation Army, where officials were to help him find temporary lodging and a job. He never showed.

Associated Press/*Orlando Sentinel*, September 3, 1987

A Broward County woman who answered a personal ad in the newspaper said she had one small task for her prospective boyfriend — to make her a widow. Sonya Walker was charged with soliciting the murder of her husband of two years, who she said mistreated her. The note with Walker's request was passed to police. A Fort Lauderdale undercover detective contacted Walker, offering to break into the house, shoot the man — making the incident look like a burglary — then rent a plane and dump the body over the Everglades. Walker said she'd then call the police and pose as a bereaved widow. When she gave the undercover officer $100 to buy a gun, she was arrested.

Associated Press/*Orlando Sentinel*, May 31, 1987

A man who told police he was a hired killer said he wasn't sure he had properly carried out his contract until his victim's body was brought into a funeral home where he worked, and he helped embalm the man. Benjamin Whitfield told police he shot into the victim's home but wasn't sure he'd done the job until the body showed up at the funeral home. The funeral home's director said Whitfield did only maintenance, and it was unlikely he could have helped in the embalming.

Associated Press/*Orlando Sentinel*, November 13, 1988

Police in North Miami charged Hugh Mack Johnson, a freelance writer, with second-degree murder after he allegedly killed his uncle and stole his violin to pay for a sex-change operation.

Palm Beach Post, December 31, 1991

EVERY BODY LOVES
FLORIDA

When a 78-year-old Gainesville woman died, her daughter didn't know what to do, so she left her on the couch. When police found the body, the daughter said the woman had been dead two years.

Orlando Sentinel, December 31, 1989

A live-in caretaker failed to report the death of an 82-year-old German citizen, then kept the body frozen in a small freezer for two years, Osceola County authorities said. The man was found frozen in an upside-down, fetal position. Police said the caretaker wanted to continue receiving her employer's $1,000 monthly railroad pension checks.

Associated Press/*St. Petersburg Times*, March 22, 1992

A man in Naples took a woman's body — packed in ice in a garbage can and loaded on the back of his pickup truck — to a lawyer. Police said the woman died of head injuries, and they were investigating the case as homicide.

St. Petersburg Times, June 8, 1989

A man who drove around with a corpse in his front seat was killed in a shoot-out with Metro-Dade police in suburban Hialeah that left two officers slightly injured. A friend called 911 after the man showed him the woman's body under some tarp and said he planned to kill an officer. The man later drove up to two officers and opened fire.

Associated Press, July 2, 1997

A call about a backed-up toilet led to the discovery of a body in a backyard septic tank in Miami.

Associated Press/*Palm Beach Post*, November 27, 1993

A body found wrapped in plastic and encased in a concrete porch at a Daytona Beach home was identified as a visitor who'd been shot in the head 15 years earlier. The police tore up the porch after receiving a tip.

Orlando Sentinel, August 14, 1993

When maids at a Fort Lauderdale hotel reported a lingering odor in room 107, police found a corpse under the bed, wrapped in plastic, surrounded by deodorant bars, and chilled by air-conditioning. A German couple had spent at least one night in the room without noticing anything. A suspect was arrested four months later.

Fort Lauderdale Sun-Sentinel, December 31, 1995

An apartment manager in St. Augustine Beach found a human brain in a bait bucket in an apartment vacated by a student.

Orlando Sentinel, December 31, 1989

Off the Northeast Florida coast, the shrimp boat *Diamond Shoal* caught an autopsied, embalmed, and bagged body in its nets. It was dressed in a two-piece suit, shirt, and tie.

Palm Beach Post, December 30, 1996

A woman whose body was found in northwestern Broward County may have been a victim of a hit-and-run accident more than 10 miles away. "We've got a scene on U.S. Highway 27 where there is not a victim, then we have a victim where there's no scene," sheriff's spokesman Jim Leljedal said.

Associated Press/*Orlando Sentinel*, January 18, 1994

When the Miami-Dade County morgue got too crowded as Miami's murder rate soared, officials began storing bodies in a refrigerated trailer truck. Later, when the morgue moved to a new, larger building, the truck was moved to the Miami-Dade County Jail, where it was used to store food for inmates.

Orlando Sentinel, January 1, 1989

Police said a Fort Myers funeral director whose licenses had been revoked and who'd been evicted for nonpayment of rent kept at least 28 bodies in cardboard boxes or caskets at a self-storage center. The center's manager called authorities when he noticed an odor coming from the end unit rented by the defunct Finley Carter Funeral Home. Supporters of the funeral director said Carter just couldn't turn people away.

Associated Press/*Palm Beach Post*, October 11, 14, 1994

A man told a Tampa funeral home director he had lost his job at a Daytona Beach funeral home because of alcoholism and wanted to sell nine cremation urns, a copying machine, a typewriter, and miscellaneous office supplies. The Tampa director gave the man $500. The items turned out to be stolen from another Tampa home; the alleged con man was a Tampa resident.

St. Petersburg Times, July 15, 1988

The children of a Palm Harbor woman gathered at a Michigan funeral home to view her casket but discovered it contained the body of someone else. Another St. Petersburg-area woman was shipped to Michigan for the first woman's funeral. The family later claimed their mother's body at a St. Petersburg funeral home. The Pinellas County Medical Examiner sent the bodies to the right place at its expense. It blamed the mixup on a private service that picks up bodies.

St. Petersburg Times, December 7, 1989

A Miami woman identified the corpse of her murdered father, paid for the funeral, and attended the open-coffin services with her family. Four months later, he showed up at her door. There had been two Alex Monroes — both 62 years old, five-foot-nine and 140 pounds, with a scar on the left side of the face. The two Monroes lived six blocks apart. The shocked daughter demanded a refund, but the funeral home agreed only to give her a credit for free services when her father really did die.

Buchanan, Edna, *Never Let Them See You Cry,* 1992.

Shortly after her murdered daughter was cremated, an Alachua County woman began having dreams that the ashes did not include those of her daughter's skull. Three years later, the woman recovered the skull, which had been sitting in the office of a University of Florida anthropologist who said he had kept it as evidence.

Associated Press/*St. Petersburg Times,* August 29, 1991

MEDICAL WONDERS

Martin County government worker Francis Reichert finally worked a cherry pit out of his nose 50 years after jamming it up a nostril while joking with friends as an eight-year-old.

Palm Beach Post, December 14, 1994

A man's glass eye popped out as he leaned over the Lake Worth Municipal Pool. He complained the eye was too small.

Palm Beach Post, February 4, 1992

An Indian Rocks Beach woman walked around for almost 24 hours with a two-inch-long sewing needle lodged in her heart after she bumped into a door at home while carrying the needle. A hospital removed the needle.

Orlando Sentinel, October 2, 1987

Fort Myers housing contractor Robert Bowers did not realize a three-inch nail was lodged in his head until it was revealed by an X ray. A coworker accidentally shot the nail from a high-powered gun while working in a development south of Fort Myers. Bowers said he felt a sharp pain several inches above his left eye but felt no pain later and believed the nail had grazed him. But his wife insisted he go to the hospital.

St. Petersburg Times, November 6, 1989

A 26-year-old Jackson County man said two assailants jumped him and cut off his private parts. He apparently placed the severed pieces in the back of his pickup and drove himself to a hospital in nearby Dothan, Alabama.

Associate Press/Orlando Sentinel, June 14, 1994

A psychic who said she had the power to undergo surgery without anesthesia claimed she lost that power after she was struck in the head at a Hollywood Home Depot store. "Now I suffer pain just like everybody else," said Penny Pellito, who sued the store.

St. Petersburg Times, January 29, 1991

A woman was critically burned after medical equipment burst into flames in her intensive care room at a Brooksville hospital. The woman was awaiting a tracheostomy — a procedure in which an opening is created in the windpipe to assist breathing. Authorities said her oxygen supply fueled the flames.

Associated Press/Miami Herald, July 3, 1991

Tampa's error-plagued University Community Hospital was stripped of the accreditation it needed to continue getting millions in federal Medicare and Medicaid money. Among the mishaps: doctors amputated the wrong leg of a diabetic man, a patient died after he was mistakenly removed from a ventilator, arthroscopic surgery was done on the wrong knee of a man, and a tubal ligation was done without a woman's consent.

Orlando Sentinel, April 14, 1995

Florida's Medical Board fined a doctor $10,000 for allegedly slapping a patient and saying, "You are going to die, and I don't care." Dr. Michael Weinberger was accused of mistreating a gunshot patient at a Lake Worth hospital, slapping the man in the face as he tried to hook up an intravenous tube, and calling him a "creep" and "pond scum." Weinberger said he was only trying to calm a combative patient.

Orlando Sentinel, June 5, 1988

A Tampa doctor was suspended after he amputated a man's toe without permission five months after cutting off the wrong leg of a previous patient. The doctor said the toe "fell off."

Fort Lauderdale Sun-Sentinel, December 30, 1995

For six years, José Cura practiced dentistry from his North Miami office, treating some 4,000 satisfied patients, all without a license. It turned out he never graduated from the University of Havana dental school, as he claimed, although he did pass both written and practical tests for his Florida license. He eventually admitted he was a fraud but displayed stacks of testimonials, hoping the state would suspend him but let him get his degree. Instead the state permanently banned him from practicing there.

Orlando Sentinel, July 10, 1988

The city of St. Petersburg, famous as a haven for the elderly, was awarded a $1,000 grant by the California Prune Board because its annual per capita prune consumption outpaced the national average by 89 percent.

Palm Beach Post, December 31, 1992

DRIVE AT YOUR OWN RISK

A woman riding in a car after a long night at a southern Miami-Dade County bar leaned out the window to vomit; her head smacked into a utility pole, killing her instantly. Her boyfriend kept driving. When a police officer finally stopped him, he said he was taking his passenger to the hospital because she was sick. "Apparently, he thought he hit a puddle," Metro-Dade police spokesman Ed Munn said, "and did not see that he'd swiped a telephone pole with her head."

Miami Herald, June 25, 1996

Josh Macias claimed he was driving on Interstate 95 in Boca Raton when a woman cut him off. He then mooned the woman, who had three children and a loaded 9-millimeter handgun in her car. The woman fired but missed. Three hours later, Macias was returning south in the same area and came across the same woman. She fired again and missed again. The chase finally ended with the woman hitting Macias' U-Haul trailer with a two-by-four. Macias was charged with a misdemeanor for the mooning, his assailant with aggravated assault.

Palm Beach Post, September 18, 1996

A driver in a Pompano Beach fender-bender leaped out of his car and began attacking people with a giant rawhide dog bone, then sprinkled them with baby powder.

Fort Lauderdale Sun-Sentinel, January 26, 1997

A nervous Delray Beach 19-year-old put her car in reverse, slammed her foot on the accelerator, and sent the car into a drainage ditch, right in the middle of her driver's license test. The car dropped into the ditch right behind the license bureau, rolling over twice and landing upside-down in two feet of muddy water. "I've heard of people having fender-benders during these tests but not this," Delray Beach police officer Kurt Eberly said. The teen and the examiner escaped injury. She didn't pass the test, but she wasn't ticketed and was told she could reapply for the test at any time. But her father said it would be a while.

Palm Beach Post, August 19, 1997

Jack and Winifred Comiskey of Chicago, ages 82 and 78, drove a rental car off the interstate in St. Petersburg and onto a runway at Albert Whitted Municipal Airport. The couple, who was not injured, said they thought they were on the expressway until they shot off the end of the runway and into Tampa Bay at about 50 miles per hour.

Orlando Sentinel, April 19, 1985

John Wesley, 69, left his Spring Hill home for the corner post office. Five days later, he called his wife from Flagstaff, Arizona, and said, "Come get me." Wesley did not know how he got there or when he ate and slept last but said he wasn't hungry and had receipts from roadside motels in four states.

St. Petersburg Times, August 12, 1992

A woman drove off from an Interstate 75 service station in Wildwood, leaving behind her 12-year-old daughter. The Alabama woman, who drove 100 miles before discovering the girl wasn't with her, said she thought the child was asleep in the back of the van.

Associated Press/*Orlando Sentinel*, July 12, 1994

A rookie Greyhound bus driver who felt sleepy pulled over in Tallahassee and told passengers, "I quit. I can't handle this any more. Does anyone have a Class B license to drive a bus?"

Associated Press/*Orlando Sentinel*, June 5, 1993

A man arguing with his wife at a Miami Dolphins game roared his Mercedes-Benz through the Pro Player Stadium parking lot, striking six people and forcing others to dive for cover.

Fort Lauderdale Sun-Sentinel, December 29, 1996

In 1994, a man repeatedly backed a car through the window of a West Palm Beach pawn shop in an effort to rob it. Police said some spectators kept urging the man on until an officer arrived and arrested him.

Palm Beach Post, January 16, 1994

A 73-year-old Sunrise man left his car to go to a newspaper rack and was walking behind it when it suddenly slipped into reverse and began careening in tight circles. The man was struck at least 10 times and was killed. A bystander was bruised when he tried to pull the keys from the moving car.

Orlando Sentinel, June 25, 1987

Eighty-nine-year-old Sol Knoll pulled out of his Century Village condominium and backed through his neighbor's living room window, knocking the neighbor from his wheelchair and over his breakfast table. Knoll first said, "I've been driving a car for about 70 years, and I never had an accident. That's a good record." After a nudge from his wife, Knoll admitted he'd had four recently.

Palm Beach Post, December 29, 1993

In 1994, 64-year-old Thelma Howard was critically injured after his wife, Dora, was startled to find a frog in her car as she pulled into the driveway. Dora proceeded to hit the gas instead of the brake, sending the car crashing into the den and pushing her husband to a far end of the room.

Palm Beach Post, December 31, 1994

In New Smyrna Beach, 1¾-year-old Travis Hendrick Jr. drove his grandfather's 1980 Oldsmobile Cutlass a quarter mile before crashing through a fence into a day-care center. His mother had gone back to the house for his car seat when Travis put the car in gear, drove down the street onto a main road, and went through the fence. As a day-care worker pulled him from the car, the boy shouted, "I drive! I drive!"

Palm Beach Post, December 31, 1992

An 18-year-old in a stolen 15-ton concrete mixing truck led police on an early-morning two-and-a-half-hour, 50-mile chase through eight Central Florida towns at speeds averaging 35 miles per hour. The truck crushed a police cruiser and a game officer's vehicle before officers stopped it by blasting two of the ten tires with shotguns. Richard Booker Branch was arrested.

Miami Herald, October 30, 1989

A Crestview police car traveling with its lights off at five A.M. struck five children sleeping on a dead-end street, killing one of them. The police chief said officers often drove with headlights off when looking for vandals and burglars. A relative said the children — ages 11 to 15 — had been kicked out of the home of a woman who was the mother of two of them.

Associated Press/*Palm Beach Post*, June 25, 1993

Two boxes of 15-inch-high, legless plastic pink flamingos dropped off a truck onto State Road 436 in Casselberry. Police collected most of the 74 birds, but some were grabbed by motorists or run over.

Orlando Sentinel, January 16, 1988

Twice in four days, 18-wheelers hauling Fruit of the Loom underwear were hijacked on Interstate 95 near Stuart.

Palm Beach Post, December 31, 1995

In 1992, in suburbs west of West Palm Beach, Domino's Pizza delivery drivers were tailing their Pizza Hut peers and offering free Domino's samples to Pizza Hut customers. Domino's corporate heads called off the competition before someone got in an accident.

Palm Beach Post, December 31, 1992

A taxi service, the police, and a funeral home combined to offer Central Florida holiday drivers who drink too much three options: a free ride home, a night in jail, or a free funeral. Officers stepped up patrols for the holiday weekend, an alcohol treatment center offered to pay for cab rides, wrecker services offered free tows, and an Orlando cemetery offered free services.

Orlando Sentinel, December 24, 1988

GOOD SPORTS

A University of Florida study said fans of the school's Gators football team believe watching a game is better than sex. A graduate student asked men and women to rate photographs, and he measured their responses with electrodes. Those who called themselves "extreme fans" registered a greater physical response to erotic photographs but rated the football images as more pleasant.

Palm Beach Post, May 10, 1997

A pair of pregame traditions landed a giant bird in handcuffs at the 1989 Florida State–Miami football game.

First the Seminoles mascot stabbed his flaming spear into the ground at the 50-yard line at Doak Campbell Stadium. Then, as Hurricanes players raced onto the field, Miami mascot, "Sebastian the Ibis," grabbed one of the fire extinguishers used to simulate storm winds and headed for the burning spear. Lawmen got to him first, slamming him against the fence and pulling his wings, uh, arms, behind his back.

"I was a defenseless bird against four cops," said Sebastian — actually John Routh. He later said he respected tradition too much to have actually doused the flame

Sebastian, the University of Miami ibis, almost wound up in jail

and demanded an apology. "He's not going to get one," Leon County Undersheriff Larry Campbell said. "He's fortunate he's not in jail."

Miami Herald, October 30, November 12, 1989

Vendor Sean Ostman, who gained fame for tossing peanuts to fans at Port St. Lucie's Thomas J. White Stadium, lost his job when an errant throw struck a Connecticut woman at a New York Mets spring training home opener in March 1993. Helen Thomas, 62, later demanded the city's insurance company pay her medical costs. Ostman had become a fan favorite for tossing the bags up to 200 feet. Later, baseball maverick Mike Veeck offered Ostman a job with the Fort Myers Miracle, but Ostman said he had no driver's license and couldn't drive to Fort Myers.

Palm Beach Post, May 9, 1993

Jacksonville's Gator Bowl suffered about $400,000 in damage in a hard freeze in 1983. So with more cold on its way and the big holiday college game looming, workers continually flushed 503 toilets for 42 hours. Each of the 23 workers was responsible for an average of 21.8 toilets.

Associated Press/Orlando Sentinel, December 28, 1989

Moments after an official heard a Deerfield Beach High soccer coach yell "waste him," two of his players sandwiched an opponent, sending the youth to the hospital on a stretcher. A jury later awarded the boy $277,000.

Fort Lauderdale Sun-Sentinel, December 31, 1995

A woman upset over criticism of her son at a youth football game in Oakland Park pulled out a gun and shot into the crowd.

Associated Press/Orlando Sentinel, November 9, 1993

When 63-year-old Michael Lenick of Sewall's Point, near Stuart, switched his television from the evening news to the Dallas Cowboys–Philadelphia Eagles football game on Halloween night in 1993, his wife, Marlene, decided she'd "had enough of that football." She went into the bedroom of their $400,000 home, got a .38-caliber handgun, and shot her husband twice. One bullet grazed his abdomen; the other went through his shoulder and neck. Police said both had been drinking. "Maybe he's a sports buff, and she never gets to watch what she wants on TV," Sewall's Point police chief Louis Savini said.

Palm Beach Post, November 22, 1993; April 22, 1995

After *Chicago Tribune* columnist Mike Royko trashed Floridians for wanting to steal his beloved White Sox and urged Chicagoans to send their dirty white socks to St.

The late Mike Royko incited Florida baseball fans

Petersburg's mayor, the *Tampa Tribune* urged readers to send orange seeds to Illinois. But officials said the mailings violated laws designed to prevent the spread of citrus canker.

Palm Beach Post, December 25, 1988

In 1993, during their inaugural season, Florida Marlins players starred in music videos that promoted Florida-grown produce. The videos showed players enjoying fresh fruit and vegetables at Joe Robbie Stadium. Trading cards featured recipes for "Home Plate Pizza," "Fast Ball Fruit Cup," and "On Deck Dunkers." On one card, Jeff Conine slugged a large tomato.

Palm Beach Post, September 9, 1993

Twelve-year-old Melissa Raglin of Boca Raton became a national symbol for women — for about four days — when she refused to wear a Babe Ruth League–mandated protective cup. Several makers of cups for females sent her free products, and the game went on.

Palm Beach Post, May 29, 1997

Fifth-grade runners from Palm Beach Gardens, training for a cross-country championship tournament in Rhode Island, practiced by running in place in the walk-in freezer at a Jupiter Italian restaurant.

Palm Beach Post, April 10, 1993

A 23-year-old Tallahassee man who hoped to get in a few holes of golf before dark was beaten with his clubs by about 10 young men. Alan Cheatwood, who suffered broken ribs, cuts, and bruises, said he was quitting the game.

Associated Press/*Miami Herald,* August 12, 1989

An angry golfer at a Tamarac course struck one partner with his club, and when the head of the club snapped off, stabbed another player with the broken end. He was charged with two counts of aggravated battery.

Associated Press/*Orlando Sentinel,* June 12, 1993

VOTING IRREGULARITIES

Shortly before running for reelection, Volusia County Councilwoman Lynne Plaskett appeared on the "Maury Povich Show" to describe how space aliens cured her terminal cancer 20 years earlier. Plaskett said a small hovering disk had entered her bedroom in Long Beach, California, levitated her body eight feet, and scanned it, then disappeared. Within four months, her cancer, which was supposed to have killed her by then, had vanished, she claimed. "I know it happened to me," she said. "I'm not ashamed of that." And, she said, "I don't think it will affect my reelection. I'm hoping the people can separate the two issues." They didn't; she lost.

Associated Press/*Palm Beach Post*, September 12, December 30, 1996

Eric A. "Rick" Kaplan, a political novice running against incumbent State Representative Bob Starks, was charged with firing five shots into Starks' Casselberry home. One struck wife, Judith Starks, in the calf as she slept. Starks, a Delta pilot, was on a flight at the time. Kaplan was later convicted. "The guy drives his own car, uses his own gun, and hides it in his own apartment," said sheriff's spokesman George Proechel. "Talk about weird —

this one takes the cake."

Palm Beach Post, September 29, 1992; Associated Press, October 14, 1997

State senate candidate Anthony "Andy" Martin was leaving the studios of the WPTV-TV station in West Palm Beach, where he'd done an interview, when a reporter began asking questions about his being wanted by authorities in New York. As tape rolled, Martin said he didn't want to talk and knocked the $40,000 camera off the photographer's shoul-

Palm Beach Post

Andy Martin doesn't like cameras

der, destroying it. Moments later he broke a microphone off another camera. Martin spent election day – a losing day for him — in jail on a hunger strike. He was later convicted and sentenced to a year in prison.

Palm Beach Post, October 31, 1996; September 19, 1997

St. Lucie County School Board candidate Karen Knapp made four spelling errors in a 23-word handwritten reply to a questionnaire for a local newspaper's editorial board. In it, she said the board should "seek local controle of schools." Later, she said her computer's spell-checker usually catches mistakes and added, "I need to be a little bit more careful."

Palm Beach Post, August 20, 1992

During Miami's 1997 mayoral election, a supporter of former Mayor Xavier Suarez was arrested, and a search of his home found more than 100 absentee ballots; at least one dead person was shown to have voted.

Later, on election day, as pollwatchers stood by, voters in a runoff picked Suarez over incumbent Joe Carollo, who immediately challenged the results. He would have won the first vote outright had he had 115 more votes.

"This makes Miami look like a Third World country," said political scientist Dario Moreno of Florida International University.

Commissioner Humberto Hernandez also won reelection overwhelmingly in 1997 despite being under indictment for conspiracy, money laundering, and fraud. The day after the election, he demanded to be sworn in immediately and even tried to swear himself in. "In my 16 years, I have never seen anything like this," city attorney Quinn Jones said. "Every year things get a little bit more bizarre here."

Palm Beach Post, November 11–13, 1997

A man ran for mayor of the small Panhandle town of Shalimar on a platform of dissolving the municipality.

Associated Press, January 26, 1993

In 1990, a 103-year-old Lake City woman registered to vote for the first time in her life. Mattie Bellamy, who had lived in Lake City since 1934, said she "just never got around" to it.

Palm Beach Post, August 7, 1990

THE PUBLIC TRUST

Miami Beach city commissioner Abe Hirschfeld spit at a *Miami Herald* reporter, saying he was symbolically striking out at the newspaper for what he called negative reporting about code violations at his oceanfront hotel. He refused to apologize and said he was proud of his actions, adding "the most powerful weapon a person can have is spitting."

Palm Beach Post, March 17, 1993

When Miami-Dade County commissioner Joe Gersten reported his Mercedes-Benz stolen from his Coral Gables driveway, four people told police it was actually nabbed outside a Miami crack house while Gersten was inside smoking crack cocaine and having sex with a prostitute. Gersten later fled, prompting a contempt of court charge. He eventually surfaced in Australia, where he sought asylum.

Miami Herald, August 14, 1997

Eugene Garrett, a judge on the Fourth District Court of Appeals, was removed from the bench after he was caught shoplifting a remote control from a Delray Beach Target store.

Palm Beach Post, February 5, 1993

Gulfport city councilman Kirby Rohrer was arrested for selling 150 grams of cocaine stashed in a Girl Scout cookie box.

Associate Press/Palm Beach Post, March 1, 1989

Montverde town council member Bill Manese was charged with aggravated battery after he attacked a neighbor with a weed trimmer, culminating a six-year property feud.

Fort Lauderdale Sun-Sentinel, June 25, 1996

State Senator Dempsey Barron, pulled over for speeding on U.S. 231 near Panama City, insisted he had just helped pass a 65-mile-per-hour speed limit. The officer reminded him his legislation was only for interstate highways, then let him go with a warning.

Palm Beach Post, December 31, 1987

State Representative Barry Silver, a Democrat from Boca Raton, got 65 traffic citations in 18 years — including three citations in 10 days — but was convicted only 13 times. In most cases, judges withheld adjudication, and the state continued to list him on his driver's license as a "safe driver."

Dempsey Barron: This law's for you, too

Palm Beach Post, November 11, 1997

Former Boynton Beach Vice Mayor Lee Wische was kicked out of a City Commission meeting when he tried to present commissioners with a "Horse's Tush Award." Wische said he represented 10 citizens looking to recognize the commission's "bumbling, bungling, and blubbery conduct of city business."

Palm Beach Post, December 31, 1991

Broward County Commissioner Gerald Thompson proposed covering the 90-foot-high mound at the county landfill with thick artificial turf and polyurethane "snow" and operating a ski slope. The head of the local snow skiing club said the place smelled too bad for anyone to try it.

Orlando Sentinel, December 10, 1987

Florida Department of Transportation director Kaye Henderson suspended himself without pay for five days for his role in padding a contract.

Palm Beach Post, December 31, 1987

THE HALLS OF POWER

The state declared September 18–24 "Meat Loaf Week."

Palm Beach Post, December 31, 1995

The Florida House took time from its busy schedule to declare Myakka Fine Sand the official state soil and Key Lime Pie the official state pie.

Palm Beach Post, December 25, 1988

Legislators passed a "potty parity" bill that ordered new and renovated buildings to have three women's toilets for every two in the men's room. Other laws proposed in the 1992 session: Youths under 18 would be banned from riding in the back of a pickup, and state money could not be used to buy Christmas cards.

Palm Beach Post, January 22, March 14, 1992

State Senator Robert Wexler, from Boca Raton, filed a bill to legalize the castration of all rapists after their second conviction. The proposal would probably be called "the Lorena Bobbitt bill," Wexler conceded. "He should move

Robert Wexler pushed to castrate rapists

to Iraq," Florida's local ACLU director, Robyn Blumner, said of Wexler.

The bill finally passed, and starting October 1, 1997, convicted sex offenders faced castration — chemical, or if the defendant chose, physical. Human rights activists called it cruel and unusual punishment, but supporters called it an effective way to stop habitual offenders. Defendants would take a drug that decreases their sex drive or could opt for the real thing.

Palm Beach Post, February 5, 1994; May 30, 1997

State Senator Dick Langley, a Republican from Clermont, sought a law that would require death row inmates to be killed the same way they killed their victims. "If he shot him in the head, he would be shot in the head. If he strangled him, he would be strangled. I think it's a really fair way to see that justice is carried out."

Orlando Sentinel, January 1, 1989

State Senator Helen Gordon Davis proposed a law that would give prostitutes the right to sue their pimps if a pimp has coerced the prostitute into the profession, caused her to remain in it, or used force to take her earnings.

Palm Beach Post, December 31, 1991

State Senator George Kirkpatrick of Gainesville said he saw no problem sponsoring one bill to declare the alligator the state reptile and another one to legalize alligator hunting.

Palm Beach Post, December 31, 1987

State Senator Jack Gordon, a Democrat from Miami, urged state lawmakers to consider a $25 fine for anyone who let a car engine idle for more than five consecutive minutes.

Palm Beach Post, December 31, 1991

YOUR GOVERNMENT
AT WORK

Visitors entering Florida on U.S. 90 near Pensacola in 1987 saw an official state highway sign that read "Welcome to Floirda." And one million official 1987 state maps placed the state capitol complex two blocks from its actual location in an inset of Tallahassee.

Palm Beach Post, December 31, 1987

Officials of the state's Division of Economic Development were embarrassed when it was revealed a promotional poster showing a Florida beach scene turned out to have been photographed in southern California.

Palm Beach Post, December 25, 1988

After the Florida Department of Law Enforcement announced a 1.7-percent drop in crime statewide from 1995 to 1996, the *Palm Beach Post* found that agencies in 20 jurisdictions had failed to submit 1996 crime reports on time. The agency simply calculated the 348,231 people in those places as having experienced no crime.

Palm Beach Post, May 11, 1997

Auditors questioned why Miami International Airport officials agreed to buy 625 new toilet seat cover devices at $8,219 each. "I have been very happy with the results in terms of customer satisfaction and the perception that Miami is now a nicer place to use the toilet," Miami-Dade County Aviation Director Gary Dellapa said. "For your home you would probably say that it is not worth it. But our toilets are very busy."

Miami Herald, December 7, 1997

After two men fishing under a Palatka bridge were drenched in sewage, the state told Amtrak to quit dumping its toilet tanks on trestles. The national rail line either dropped waste directly on tracks or into a holding tank, which was dumped when trains reached 25 miles per hour. Amtrak said it never dumped directly into the St. Johns River.

The state backed off after Amtrak threatened to suspend service in Florida. The company, meanwhile, said it was looking into refitting cars, but said it would cost $85 million.

Palm Beach Post, June 13, 1989; November 23, 1991

An engineer relying on a 1950s map designed a Lantana toll plaza two feet into a drainage canal that wasn't shown on the map. Florida's turnpike officials had to spend $319,000 to reroute the canal.

Palm Beach Post, July 3, 1989

A flyer distributed by Central Florida postal authorities urged residents to help carriers by clearing ice and snow from their steps.

Calamity Calendar, 1990

Nearly 10,000 pounds of undelivered mail, some three years old, was found in the yard of a Pensacola mail carrier. Most of the mail was third-class junk mail, including sweepstake pitches and diaper samples. Postal officials said none of the carrier's 500 customers complained of missing any mail.

Orlando Sentinel, January 1, 1989

In 1992, it was disclosed that only three of Palm Beach County's 38 towns complied with a 1959 state statute requiring local governments to name backup officials in the event of a nuclear holocaust.

Palm Beach Post, December 31, 1992

An executive recruiter who was paid $26,500 to help the Palm Beach County Health Care District find a new executive director submitted the following candidates: a psychologist whose license was revoked for having a social relationship with a client, a man forced to resign from a job for lying about his bachelor's degree, and a former health-care consultant from Arizona forced to resign from his job because of low morale among his employees.

Palm Beach Post, December 31, 1992

Firefighters in the Broward County town of Margate built their new firehouse too small for their truck. They had to spend another $65,000 in renovations to get the truck inside.

Orlando Sentinel, January 1, 1989

An Oviedo couple was surprised when their July 1988 water bill said they used 305,000 gallons — nearly 20 times their normal amount. The city said tests showed the meter to be 99 percent accurate and the couple had to pay the $215.90. The previous high bill was $25.50 for 33,000 gallons.

Orlando Sentinel, January 11, 1989

A Medicare computer declared John Gunning of suburban Lake Worth dead and refused to reimburse him for a $51 hospital bill.

Palm Beach Post, December 31, 1991

When Joanna Grun of West Palm Beach mistakenly wrote a check for $17.36 for a doctor's visit that should have cost $17.35, Medicare spent 18 cents to send her a check for a penny. A health insurance specialist explained that reprogramming the system to stop cutting minuscule checks would cost too much.

Palm Beach Post, December 29, 1993

A Bayonet Point man got a one-cent bill for back taxes along with a $10 penalty fee.

Associated Press/*Orlando Sentinel,* August 1, 1993

A "toll-free" hotline set up by the state to help single mothers trying to collect child support from deadbeat dads ended up billing the mothers as much as 67 cents a minute. The state deducted the mothers' telephone fees from any child support payments collected.

Orlando Sentinel, January 1, 1989

Broward County school officials proposed banning the wearing of sunglasses in school, claiming that glasses hid the bloodshot eyes of stoned students.

Palm Beach Post, December 25, 1988

A staffer at the state Department of Business and Professional Regulation was investigated after her bosses claimed she'd been practicing voodoo rituals at work.

Palm Beach Post, December 31, 1994

When Jacksonville passed an ordinance requiring all tickets for a Beastie Boys concert bear the warning "for mature audiences," the group challenged the ordinance's constitutionality in federal court, and the city was ordered to pay $1,000. The city council approved the warning after hearing that shows featured a 21-foot phallus, a band member mooning the audience, and the group urging female concert-goers to bare their breasts.

Orlando Sentinel, January 1, 1989

Highlights of letters sent to Broward County mayors:

✘ A Tamarac woman said her Martian neighbors wouldn't throw out their garbage.

✘ A New Jersey woman told Hallandale's mayor her family had been watched by a satellite that could even read her brain waves.

✘ A part-time Cooper City resident said police followed him back to Canada each year and watched him with an X-ray machine.

✘ A Pembroke Pines woman said a spacecraft that had kidnapped her husband two years earlier also picked her up, then dropped her off at home.

St. Petersburg Times, May 13, 1989

U.S. Customs and Secret Service agents in Miami used a steamroller to publicly crush 17,000 seized fake Rolex, Concord, and Piaget wristwatches.

Orlando Sentinel, January 1, 1989

The post office in Ochopee — a town out in the Big Cypress — is eight feet, four inches by seven feet, three inches, and 10½ feet high. It's America's smallest post office. In fact, the building, about the size of a garden shed, is just about the whole town.

Palm Beach Post, May 26, 1991

RESOURCES

City Libraries: Boca Raton, Belray Beach, Boynton Beach, West Palm Beach

County Libraries: Miami–Dade County, Broward County, Palm Beach County

University Libraries: Florida Atlantic, Florida State, Florida International, West Florida

Historical Societies: Florida, South Florida, Palm Beach, Broward County, Hollywood

Florida State Archives

Florida Photographic Archives

Florida Handbook by Allen Morris

Some stories in this book originally appeared as articles in the *Palm Beach Post*:

Undying Love: October 29, 1995
The Ghost of Flight 401: October 29, 1995
Flame On: October 29, 1995
UFOs Over Gulf Breeze: August 2, 1996
The Koreshan: October 14, 1987; March 14, 1993
Coral Castle: February 13, 1994
The Bardin Booger: October 31, 1989
Spook Hill: November 20, 1994
The Bat Tower: June 27, 1993
The Snake Man: June 10, 1990
"History Ain't Pretty: Bloopers, Bozos, and Blunders in Florida's Past" was adapted from a talk to the Florida Historical Society annual convention on May 10, 1991, and a May 21, 1991, article in the *Palm Beach Post*.

Primary Sources for *The Daily Weird*:

Palm Beach Post
Fort Lauderdale Sun-Sentinel
Miami Herald
Orlando Sentinel
St. Petersburg Times
Tampa Tribune
The Associated Press
Sheperd, Chuck, John J. Kohut, and Roland Sweet. *News of the Weird*. New York: Penguin Books, 1989.
Sheperd, Chuck, John J. Kohut, and Roland Sweet. *More News of the Weird*. New York: Penguin Books, 1990.
Buchanan, Edna. *Never Let Them See You Cry*. New York: Random House, 1992.